Defining Terrorism

Abir Taha

DEFINING TERRORISM:

The End of Double Standards

Towards a Universal Definition of Terrorism

ARKTOS
London 2014

First edition published in 2014 by Arktos Media Ltd.

ISBN 978-1-907166-83-9

BIC Classification:
Terrorism law (LNFV)
Palestine (1FBP)
Israel (1FBH)

Layout and Cover: Tor Westman

ARKTOS MEDIA LTD.
www.arktos.com

CONTENTS

To my father and all the
victims of terrorism

TERRORISM:
THE NEED FOR A UNIVERSAL DEFINITION

Terrorism constitutes, in the post-Cold War era, arguably the most serious challenge and threat to international peace and security. This monster's ugly tentacles reach the four corners of the planet with indiscriminate ruthlessness, murdering and maiming innocent civilians everywhere, from Bali to Baghdad, from Kabul to London, from Moscow to Beirut. Nothing justifies terrorism. Nothing should justify terrorism. The noblest cause turns into an abomination when it is sullied by terrorism. That is why international humanitarian law condemns this modern plague as a crime against humanity.

The unspeakable horror of the diabolical terror machine reached its peak in the attacks of 11 September 2001, when thousands of men, women, and children from all nationalities and walks of life lost their lives, and thousands of others were scarred — both physically and emotionally — for life. Yet these terrible attacks, far from achieving the plotters and perpetrators' objectives of spreading terror and chaos, have instead only strengthened the international community's firm resolve to eradicate the scourge of terrorism permanently.

Nevertheless, the so-called 'war on terror', a kind of Third World War waged by the United States and sanctioned by its allies from both East and West immediately after 11 September, has not been able to eliminate this global menace, for it remains a selective, incomplete, and ineffective war so long as it is not based on a general consensus regarding the definition of terrorism.

With the absence of such a consensus on what exactly constitutes a terrorist act — regardless of the target chosen by a terrorist group and the identity of its perpetrators — the 'war on terror' is doomed to fail drastically unless a universal definition of terrorism is adopted by the international community at large. Indeed, terrorism is an international problem that can only be resolved by the international community. No single country or even superpower can impose its own definition of 'terrorism' on the others.

Hitherto, the subject of terrorism has been frequently discussed, debated, used — and abused — by states to condemn, accuse and punish their enemies and their agents, yet a clear, permanent, universal, comprehensive, internationally-recognised, and United Nations-promulgated definition is still missing. The result is chaos, confusion and controversy surrounding this delicate and crucial subject. Examples of such disagreements on the use of the term 'terrorist' are legion: Hezbollah, Hamas, the Revolutionary Armed Forces of Colombia (FARC), the Irish Republican Army (IRA), Basque Homeland and Freedom (ETA), the Taliban, the Tamil Tigers, and so on: are these 'terrorists' or 'freedom fighters'?

Why all this confusion when it comes to pinpointing who is a terrorist? The confusion lies in the definition — or rather, the absence of a definition — of terrorism. Indeed, hitherto, the definition of terrorism that has been used in international relations has been mainly political, relative, partial, shifting, and selective.

Whereas the sweeping majority of states condemn terrorism *per se* — at least publicly — in all its forms as totally inacceptable or at least highly objectionable, they remain deeply divided on providing a definitive definition of terrorism and of the methods to combat it, a fact which renders terrorism one of the most divisive, controversial and problematic issues in contemporary international affairs. It is a highly sensitive subject of contention and controversy that hampers relations between states and makes the fight against terrorism selective and arbitrary, serving the national interests and aims of particular states rather than being global in scope and truly defeating this modern plague.

The current controversy surrounding the issue of terrorism undermines international relations and weakens the legitimacy of international law, for it leads to different, often diverging, ideas about and interpretations of terrorism.

Significant legal steps have been taken by the international community to combat terrorism: the International Court of Justice (ICJ) condemned all forms of terrorism and terrorist attacks, and at least twelve conventions against terrorism have been endorsed by the United Nations. Countless resolutions condemning terrorism have been adopted by the international body, including Security Council resolution 1373 of September 2001 and 1269 of October 1999, which both denounce 'all acts, methods and practices of terrorism as criminal and unjustified, regardless of their motivation'.

Nevertheless — and sadly — none of these conventions and resolutions defines the word 'terrorism'. So how can terrorism be combated in a fair and efficient manner, if it is not first identified?

This flagrant absence of a unified definition of terrorism has been particularly felt in the aftermath of the attacks of 11 September, a fact that makes the need for such a definition more pressing and essential than ever before, especially after the so-called 'Arab Spring' which, instead of ushering in the dawn of a new democratic and liberal era in the Middle East, has instead witnessed the proliferation of obscurantist and fundamentalist groups who commit unspeakable atrocities against civilians based solely on their religious identity and political affiliation. The peoples of the Middle East are just awakening from their dream of the 'Arab Spring' to find out that this dream has turned into an Islamist nightmare in a region where terrorism of the worst kind thrives, sponsored, armed, equipped, and financed by regional and international powers.

Hence, in order to eradicate terrorism, a consensus must be reached on what the term actually means. Only a truly universal and comprehensive definition that meets the general approval of all states will safeguard against double standards in identifying and fighting terrorism, and will thus ensure universal justice.

Yet what constitutes a terrorist act? Is it simply an attack on innocent civilians? Does the target of the attack or the identity of the perpetrators matter, as is presently the case, in qualifying an act as 'terrorist'? Shouldn't rather all terrorist acts be condemned, irrespective of any other considerations?

Moreover, why is it that only individuals and sub-national groups are accused of terrorism, despite the fact that international law also clearly and firmly condemns state terrorism (General Assembly resolution 39/159 of 17 December 1984), and, taking into consideration that most major terrorist acts have been committed — or sponsored — by states?

That is why defining terrorism should be high on the list of priorities for the UN, since doing so will put an end to the controversy surrounding this overly politicised term and to the double standards that have characterised — and continue to characterise — international relations.

I

Defining Terrorism: Conditions and Criteria for Consensus

By nature, terrorism is difficult to define, mainly because the term has been arbitrarily used as a political accusation — instead of a legal indictment — by states to describe the acts of their enemies, and therefore its definition lacks the legal aspect, which is needed to truly make it universal. States have frequently thrown accusations of terrorism at each other, a fact which has made the 'war on terrorism' all but lose its credibility and legitimacy.

Thus arises the necessity to set the conditions and criteria for a truly universal and permanent definition of terrorism, in compliance with General Assembly resolution 42/159 of 7 December 1987, which recognises that 'the effectiveness of the struggle against terrorism could be enhanced by the establishment of a generally agreed definition of international terrorism'.

For a definition to be officially and universally adopted, it must meet certain conditions and criteria. Therefore, the following are needed in order to reach a consensus:

1. The definition should be legal and permanent

There is an urgent need for a clear definition of terrorism that is applied consistently, i.e. a legal definition that is permanent, not a political one that changes frequently to suit the interests of certain states or superpowers. Indeed, a scrutiny of international events reveals that states do not judge terrorism as much by the actual act of violence as by who is the target of this violent activity, as well as by the identity of the perpetrators of such acts.

The old adage, 'one man's terrorist is another man's freedom fighter', is more relevant than ever in the current international debate and in the global so-called 'war against terrorism' or 'war on terror'. The question of 'who is a terrorist?' and 'who is a freedom fighter?' will undoubtedly persist so long as the political aspect still dominates the issue.

Numerous examples testify to the total confusion and controversy surrounding this politically-motivated, relative and highly volatile definition: first among these examples is al-Qaeda, which is by all standards a purely terrorist organisation targeting innocent civilians. Or so it should be considered, but this is not always so.

Indeed, the people who would later form the Taliban, as well as Osama bin Laden, were praised as *mujahideen*, or 'freedom fighters', and backed by the US and its Arab and Western allies, when they were resisting the Soviet occupation of Afghanistan. Two decades later, as the horrific attacks of 11 September were claimed by al-Qaeda's leader Osama bin Laden, the US branded both groups as terrorist and bin Laden became the world's most wanted terrorist, his network becoming the main target of the 'war against terrorism' which is still ongoing to this day.

This same al-Qaeda was behind many of the attacks which cost the lives of—or permanently maimed—countless American soldiers in Iraq. However, following the 'Arab Spring', the national interests of the major powers shifted in the region and a number of Western and Arab states began arming, training, and financing al-Qaeda and its surrogate, the al-Nusra Front, in Syria, as well as other radical Islamist groups like the 'Islamic State in Iraq and Levant', which is fighting the secular Syrian regime of Bashar al-Assad. The irony and the paradox lie in the fact that these same Western powers are simultaneously fighting al-Qaeda terrorists in Afghanistan, in central Africa and in Mali, whilst supporting them in Syria...

Another example of the changing, politicised and relative definition of terrorism is the Turkish-Kurdish conflict. The Turks accuse Kurdish separatists and their former leader, Abdullah Ocalan, of being 'terrorists', yet this same Ocalan was (and is still seen) seen as a Kurdish hero by his followers and by most of the world, a freedom fighter engaged in a legitimate struggle to achieve Kurdish national self-determination.

A third example of such a volatile definition of terrorism is the Palestinian case and cause. The Palestinians, who have been engaged in a decades-long legitimate resistance to end Israel's unlawful occupation of their land, are freedom fighters in the eyes of most of the world and according to both international law and UN resolutions, yet Israel and its ally, the US, are virtually the only countries in the world that label Palestinian resistance fighters as 'terrorists'.

In yet another example which illustrates the highly politicised and selective definition of terrorism, Israel, the US, and lately the European Union have accused Lebanon's Hezbollah of being a 'terrorist' organisation, while the latter is viewed by the Lebanese people and most of the international community as a legitimate resistance group whose heroic military actions against the Israeli occupation forces ousted the latter from Lebanon in 2000 and defeated them again in 2006 during Israel's war of aggression, Lebanon thus becoming the only country to actually defeat the self-proclaimed 'invincible' Israeli army.

As seen above, politically motivated definitions of terrorism focus not on the terrorist act itself—as they should—but instead on its target and on the identity of the perpetrators, and accordingly the states making these biased definitions decide whether the act should be condemned or condoned.

In contrast to this selective and fickle definition, the legal definition of terrorism should be permanent and consistent, condemning any terrorist act wherever and whenever it occurs. Terrorism is purely and simply the unlawful use of force, and the use of violence targeting civilians and aimed at spreading terror among the public. No other considerations—especially political ones—should interfere in defining terrorism.

2. The definition should be universal

In order to achieve consensus and avoid controversy, the definition of terrorism should be universal, i.e. it should meet the general approval of the international community and be endorsed by a vast majority of the UN member states, and thus have a binding, coercive and punitive effect on all.

To achieve this universality, the United Nations, which is the only organisation representing the world community, should therefore be the sole authority to define terrorism, and the only legal and political umbrella for any counter-terrorist resolutions or measures, as well as of any 'international coalition' against terrorism.

No single state or superpower should be allowed to create its own partial and biased definition of terrorism and accordingly condemn its enemies as 'terrorists', threatening military intervention in the domestic affairs of other states or sponsoring its own network of terrorists against other states. State sovereignty should remain a main principle of international law, and should only be superseded by international humanitarian law when actual human rights violations have been perpetrated by a state against its own citizens. However, these violations should be proven to be real, not fabrications to be used as a rationale to interfere in the internal affairs of other states.

Simply accusing a state without solid and objective evidence of 'human rights violations against its own people' has become a nefarious trend in post-11 September international relations and a common means to interfere in sovereign states' internal affairs; it has become the best excuse and weapon to topple regimes that are deemed 'unfriendly' to major powers and their interests.

Significant steps should also be taken to ensure that all states sign and implement all international conventions and UN resolutions which oppose international terrorism, in conformity with UN General Assembly resolution 44/29 of 4 December 1989, which urges states 'to take promptly all steps necessary to implement the existing international conventions on this subject [terrorism] to which they are parties, including the harmonisation of their domestic legislation with those conventions', and 'appeals to all states that have not yet done so to consider becoming party to international conventions relating to various aspects of international terrorism'.

That includes UN resolutions condemning state terrorism, in order to avoid a selective endorsement and implementation of resolutions and conventions against terrorism and of measures to combat terrorism, as was the case, to cite but one example, on 7 December 1987, when only two states—the United States and Israel—rejected UN General Assembly resolution 42/159 condemning the occupation of Palestinian territories and upholding the right of peoples to self-determination and the legitimacy of national liberation movements, a resolution that was approved by 153 other states (with one abstention).

In this context, an international conference on international terrorism should be held under the UN banner in an attempt to reach a unified definition of terrorism, in conformity with UN General Assembly resolution 42/159, which calls for such a consensus, and in accordance with UN General Assembly resolution 44/29.

Following the international conference, the UN should issue a resolution defining terrorism and set up a specialised legal mechanism whose function it will be to endorse the new definition of terrorism, implement anti-terrorism measures, and institutionalise international cooperation in the fight against terrorism. All amendments to the definition should also be made under UN supervision and subject to its approval.

3. The definition should be comprehensive

The most efficient way to fight and eliminate terrorism is to apply global justice; that is, there should be a universal jurisdiction in the war against terrorism, not selective 'justice' applied unilaterally and arbitrarily by certain states against what they perceive as 'terrorist' targets.

Therefore, in order to avoid double standards, the definition of terrorism should include and condemn *all* forms and acts of terrorism, wherever and by whomever they are committed, irrespective of the identity of the perpetrator or the target; that includes individuals, groups, and states that practice or sponsor all kinds of terrorism, whether domestic, regional, or international in scope.

Any attack against innocent civilians constitutes a terrorist act, regardless of the nationality or political affiliation of those behind the attack as well as the nationality or political affiliation of the victims of such attacks.

The need for a comprehensive definition of terrorism had already been underlined by UN General Assembly resolution 44/29, which calls for 'measures to prevent international terrorism' and which unequivocally condemns as 'criminal and unjustifiable' all acts, methods and practices of terrorism, 'wherever and by whomever committed'.

In this context, terrorist acts clearly fall into the category of crimes against humanity and should therefore be unambiguously referred to as such, for these acts, whether in the form of murder, occupation, hostage-taking, torture, and so on are identical in every way to crimes against humanity.

4. The definition should condemn state terrorism as the highest form of terrorism

International law condemns terrorism in all its forms; that includes terrorism perpetrated by individuals and sub-national groups, but it also covers state terrorism and state-sponsored terrorism. Thus arises the need to apply international law to all these categories without preference or discrimination; hence, in order to ensure a comprehensive definition of terrorism that encompasses all forms of terrorism, the definition should include and condemn state terrorism as well as individual or group terrorism.

What is state terrorism? It is the unlawful use of violence or repression perpetrated by a state against some or all of its citizens, based on political, social, racial, religious, or cultural discrimination, or against the citizens of a territory occupied or annexed by the said state, or those of other countries. State terrorism also includes — and takes the form of — state-sponsored terrorism against other states, through the financing, arming, and equipping of terrorist groups that target state institutions as well as innocent civilians.

State terrorism is the highest form of terrorism because it is organised, legalised, and institutionalised terrorism which is implemented by a state apparatus and its agents.

5. The definition should clearly distinguish between terrorism & resistance

The vast majority of states condemn terrorism in all its forms, regarding it as being without any justification; yet as long as a unified, comprehensive and universal definition which applies to all is still lacking, the problem of assigning the label 'terrorist' to the right — instead of presumed — culprits, whether individuals, groups or states, will linger.

In other words, terrorism should first be clearly defined before it is combated, in order to avoid branding as 'terrorism' legitimate and righteous activities such as resistance to foreign occupation or the struggle for self-determination, as is often the case nowadays. Terrorist acts should be denounced regardless of the identity of the perpetrator or the target, provided the acts themselves are terroristic in nature and do not constitute part of a national resistance.

An example of this confusion between these two antithetical themes — terrorism and resistance — is the statement made in 2002 by the then newly-appointed US deputy assistant Secretary of State, David Satterfield, in which he equated the *Intifada*, which embodies legitimate Palestinian popular resistance to the illegitimate Israeli occupation, with 'terrorism', describing this civilian uprising as a 'process of calculated terror' These words not only show a complete ignorance — or denial — of undeniable facts on the ground, (namely, that the Israeli occupation forces are the ones using methods of terror against unarmed Palestinian youths), but they also show a blatant contempt for all international conventions and UN resolutions which clearly advocate the right of peoples to self-determination.

Likening movements that resist Israeli occupation from Shebaa (a Lebanese territory still under Israeli occupation), to the occupied Golan, to the West Bank, to a purely terroristic organisation like al-Qaeda represents a total lack of respect for the UN Charter as well as international law, which firmly uphold the right of a people to resist foreign occupation by all means.

In spite of the Americans' official opposition to resistance movements, most of the international community recognises that the struggle of the Palestinian people is an honourable fight to achieve statehood and their legitimate right, and that Hezbollah attacks against Israeli occupation forces in southern Lebanon were not terrorism but national resistance.

Such confusion between terrorism and resistance stems from a flawed definition of terrorism that emphasises non-state actors and downplays state terrorism, and thus fails to differentiate between terrorism properly called as such, and a struggle for national liberation, such as the resistance operations carried out by the Palestine Liberation Organisation (PLO) and later by Hamas against Israel, which is aimed at ending Israeli occupation and achieving national self-determination for the Palestinian people.

As shown above, recorded history — which is selective, often differing radically from historical facts — has mainly focused on terrorism that is aimed against governments, not paying heed to state terrorism. Yet, upon closer investigation, it is evident that even acts of violence that are committed by state authorities can also be terroristic in nature, as for example, state-sponsored terrorism. Consequently, terrorism is not necessarily the same thing as violence against a government, and the term 'terrorism' is not to be confused with guerrilla war, riots, and so forth.

Thus there is an urgent and crucial need to distinguish between terrorism proper and the legitimate struggle for national liberation and self-determination of peoples. Resistance and terrorism not only differ from each other, they are antithetical issues, and any attempt to link them only serves dubious political objectives.

Upholding the legitimacy of national resistance: A UN list of national liberation movements

In order to distinguish between resistance and terrorism and to avoid any arbitrary, selective, and politically-motivated labelling of states or groups as terrorists, as well as to give resistance groups and freedom fighters an international legal status and legitimacy, and hence international support and protection, a comprehensive list of national liberation movements in the world should be established under the supervision, and with the approval of, the United Nations. This exhaustive list is to be contrasted with the list of individuals, groups and states practising terrorism, in order to draw a clear and permanent distinction between these two categories.

II

State Terrorism and State-Sponsored Terrorism: The Highest Form of terrorism

State terrorism and international law's double standards

In order to protect the sacrosanct sovereignty of states and serve their interests, the general tendency of international law has been to disregard — in practice, not in theory, state terrorism being explicitly condemned by international conventions — terrorism that is practised by states, mainly because states are the major actors in the international arena, and are therefore not keen to denounce their own unlawful actions.

Indeed, as an example of the nations' reluctance to denounce state terrorism, the US State Department's definition of terrorism as 'premeditated, politically motivated violence perpetrated against non-combatant targets by sub-national groups or clandestine agents, usually intended to influence an audience' (Title 22 of the United States Code, Section 2656f[d]), restricts terrorism to sub-national groups, i.e. a grouping not recognised as a nation-state, ignoring — and thus implicitly condoning — state terrorism.

Yet in clear contrast to the State Department's definition of terrorism, states have, and continue, to use violence and terror against their enemies in order to accomplish a particular premeditated political goal. Consequently, terrorism is by no means solely practised by non-state actors. Although there has been some mention of state-sponsored terrorism in the US State Department in past decades, there is still no recognition that states can actually be perpetrators of terrorism.

The term 'terrorist state', which was later introduced into the State Department's definition of terrorism, refers only to countries that sponsor terrorist groups and does not mention, let alone condemn, the actual and direct use of terrorism by a state. Thus there is a clear intention by states not to include state terrorism in their definition of, or fight against, terrorism. This situation cannot endure if we are to reach a comprehensive definition that includes all entities practising terrorism without any arbitrary and unjust distinctions.

How is it that terrorism came to mean only individual or group terrorism, and not state terrorism? Most often international law reflects the particular interests of certain regional or international powers and is thus manipulated to serve their particular interests. If we trace the origin and evolution of the word 'terrorism' throughout history, we might understand the underlying causes behind this negligence: the word 'terrorism' was first used during the French Revolution, when the state violently repressed the civilian population during the Jacobins' 'reign of terror'; terrorism back then meant terror by the state against its own citizens.

It was only much later that the word 'terrorist' came to mean, according to the modern definition set forth by the Oxford dictionary, 'a member of a clandestine or expatriate organisation aiming to coerce an established government by acts of violence against its subjects', changing the word's meaning to only that of terror committed by individuals and sub-national groups against a state, while ignoring any terrorist activity perpetrated by a state.

In 1937, the League of Nations completely twisted the term's meaning, defining terrorism as 'criminal acts directed against a state and intended or calculated to create a state of terror in the minds of particular persons or the general public'. When states set out to formulate a definition of terrorism, the latter will naturally and clearly imply that terrorism can only be perpetrated by non-state actors.

The first recorded usage of terrorism in this sense was in 1947, in the British Annual Register in reference to the attack on the King David hotel in Jerusalem, which condemned 'the latest and worst of the outrages committed by the Jewish terrorists in Palestine'. But when the Israelis unilaterally declared their statehood the next year amid international consternation, they were careful not to use that word in reference to their founders.

From 1968 to 1978, the period that came to be known as the 'decade of terror', historical records solely refer to the 'terrorism' practised by the Red Army Faction, the Red Brigades, the ETA, the PLO, the IRA, and so forth, and not to violence perpetrated by states. It is as though a tacit agreement was made between states not to denounce any terrorism perpetrated by states, thus implicitly condoning — and turning a blind eye to — each other's state terrorism.

Nowadays, when governments use methods of terror, this terror is not seen as a threat to the existing status quo, but is rather described as 'maintaining law and order'. Thus there are two forms of terrorism: that which is used by the state, and that which is used against it; only the latter one is branded 'terrorism' by states, while state terrorism is allowed to go unpunished.

The fact that during the 1980s, state-sponsored terrorism was widespread throughout the world did nothing to change this biased definition or the double standards used in implementing international law.

'Terrorism', in the sense it is used today, thus means acts of violence in support of political goals...except when committed by a government. This biased, one-sided definition has dangerous implications; indeed, giving governments a monopoly on violence is a clear violation of international law. From this standpoint, why were Nazi Germany and Fascist Italy's actions branded 'state terrorism' and 'crimes against humanity', whereas, decades later, Israel continues to violate every UN resolution and international convention on a daily basis through its state terrorism against Palestinians?

It is a morally and legally unacceptable fact that Israel, as a state, is allowed to remain unaccountable and go unpunished for its crimes, whereas Palestinian fighters, who have been bereft of their legitimate right to statehood, are labelled as 'terrorists' by Israeli authorities, and even stone-throwing Palestinian children are arrested and tortured for resisting the occupation of their ancestral land.

This clearly shows that, in current international affairs, it is the actor's identity, and not the act itself, which determines whether the term 'terrorism' should be applied; thus, theoretically, terrorism is always attributed to the state's official enemies and never to the state itself or its allies.

As demonstrated above, although state terrorism greatly predates the problem of international terrorism committed by groups, it remains virtually and purposely unnoticed by the international community. Conversely, according to some aspects of international law, Palestinian resistance to Israeli terrorism could be interpreted as 'internal rebellion'. It is a complete double standard, intended to serve state interests, yet widely recognised by most states. This constitutes a dangerous flaw in international law, and threatens its credibility and legitimacy and undermines justice, as well as international peace and security.

State terrorism: the highest form of terrorism

As we have seen above, to this day, the label 'terrorist' has mainly been confined — in the realm of international affairs, at least — to individuals or groups practising terrorism, not to states, despite the fact that state terrorism is the highest form of terrorism, being legitimised and justified by domestic law and being committed by the state's official apparatus, i.e. organised, state-sanctioned terrorism. This politically-motivated negligence does not change the fact that, in theory at least, international law and UN resolutions firmly condemn state terrorism.

Despite the flagrant double standards used by the international community in applying international law, unlawful acts committed by states are strictly prohibited by the United Nations: state responsibility in directly supporting such acts is a fully established principle under customary international law.

International law firmly condemns state terrorism, as the following UN resolutions show:

1. General Assembly resolution 44/29 on 'measures to prevent international terrorism' unequivocally condemns as 'criminal and unjustifiable' all acts, methods and practices of terrorism, 'wherever and by whomever committed', which implies that none are — or should be — above the law when it comes to combating terrorism: neither non-state actors nor state officials.
2. In a more direct reference to terrorism that is practised by states, General Assembly resolution 39/159 of 17 December 1984, on the 'inadmissibility of the policy of state terrorism

> and any actions by states aimed at undermining the socio-political system in other sovereign states' reaffirms 'the obligation of all states to refrain in their international relations from the threat or use of force against the sovereignty, territorial integrity and political independence of any State', and 'resolutely condemns policies and practices of terrorism in relations between states as a method of dealing with other states and peoples', demanding that 'all States take no actions aimed at military intervention and occupation, forcible change in or undermining of the socio-political system of States, destabilisation and overthrow of their Governments and, in particular, initiate no military action to that end under any pretext whatsoever and cease forthwith any such action already in progress'. There can be no clearer and stronger condemnation of state terrorism by the United Nations than this.

As we have seen above, the recorded history of international relations has focused mainly on terrorism in the form of violence against a government. Yet, upon closer investigation, it is apparent to any objective observer or analyst that even acts of violence which originate in state governments, or in their authorities, can be terrorism, as, for example, state-inspired or state-sponsored terrorism. States are in fact the biggest sponsors and perpetrators of terrorism.

A quick glance at contemporary world history shows us that, if we simply look at acts of terrorism in themselves and not at the perpetrators of such acts, and even according to the definitions employed by the US State Department, the Central Intelligence Agency (CIA), and the Federal Bureau of Investigation (FBI), states — not individuals or groups — have been the biggest sponsors and perpetrators of international terrorism.

As an example, during the Cold War, both the USA and the Soviet Union gave covert support — directly or indirectly - to revolutionary movements seeking to overthrow regimes allied to the opposing side. The CIA helped to finance and arm many terrorist organisations such as the Afghan rebels and other violent revolutionary groups. This historical fact casts doubt on the credibility of the ongoing 'war against terrorism', which has become a misnomer with the outbreak of the Syrian armed conflict, given that the same Western and Arab states — the USA, Great Britain, France, Saudi Arabia, Qatar, and Turkey, to name only the major ones — that pretend to fight terrorism are also directly financing, arming and sponsoring Salafist Takfiri terrorist groups that are terrorising and killing scores of civilians in Syria on a daily basis.

States — with a few exceptions — have hitherto been immune to the jurisdiction of international law, protected by the UN's sacrosanct principle of national sovereignty, yet this immunity has ceased to be absolute, gradually giving in to the emerging authority of international humanitarian law, especially in the aftermath of the first Gulf War and the recent 'Arab Spring'.

The universal principle of human rights has taken the lead and, following the Nuremberg tribunal and the ensuing Geneva Conventions, with their notions of 'crimes against humanity', 'war crimes', and 'crimes of genocide', have lifted the immunity of state officials accused of such criminal acts, and have sanctioned the intervention — on humanitarian grounds — in the internal affairs of states in case the latter are in clear and proven violation of their own citizens' human rights or those of neighbouring countries.

The trials of Slobodan Milošević, Augusto Pinochet, and Saddam Hussein, among others, as well as the unsuccessful attempts to try Israeli Prime Minister Ariel Sharon for his responsibility in the massacre of Palestinian civilians in the Sabra and Shatila refugee camps, are but clear indications of this qualitative and significant shift in international law.

International humanitarian law now prevails, albeit in theory, over state sovereignty, and although states continue to enjoy relative freedom to conduct violent and repressive policies against their own citizens or those of other countries, legally they are nonetheless prohibited from transgressing human rights.

The trial of Milošević has broken a taboo, that of the supremacy of state sovereignty, and it is only a matter of time before the trial of other notorious war criminals will follow suit, if international law is to restore its legitimacy and credibility among the world community.

State officials today are no longer above the law, and they are now liable to be prosecuted; there is no immunity for war criminals — at least in theory — in the new world order. However, as stated above, the only danger lies in states using the pretext of international humanitarian law and the 'protection of civilians' to justify their interference in other states' internal affairs, as was the case with the outright Western aggression against Libya. Nonetheless, international humanitarian law is now an integral part of international law and no single state is allowed to practice terrorism against its own citizens or against the citizens of occupied states.

Forms of state terrorism

1. Occupation: the highest form of state terrorism

Foreign military occupation and/or forced annexation of land or property — whether as a result of aggression, war, or invasion, or in the form of illegal settlement building — is condemned by international law as an unlawful act of violence, a crime against international peace and security, and a flagrant breach of the sovereignty and territorial integrity of the occupied or annexed state.

Occupation is thus a form of terrorism, because it involves political violence against innocent people, an act that is denounced by UN General Assembly resolution 44/29, which unequivocally condemns as 'criminal and unjustifiable' 'all acts, methods and practices of terrorism, wherever and by whomever committed'.

In this context, General Assembly resolution 39/159 on the 'inadmissibility of the policy of state terrorism and any actions by states aimed at undermining the socio-political system in other sovereign states' clearly condemns state terrorism and reaffirms 'the obligation of all states to refrain in their international relations from the threat or use of force against the sovereignty, territorial integrity and political independence of any State'.

This resolution labels occupation a form of state terrorism, urging all states to 'take no actions aimed at military intervention and occupation, forcible change in or undermining of the socio-political system of States, destabilisation and overthrow of their Governments and, in particular, initiate no military action to that end under any pretext whatsoever and cease forthwith any such action already in progress'.

2. Crimes against humanity

The violent, premeditated, and destructive nature of terrorist acts makes them fall under the category of crimes against humanity described in Article 7 of the International Criminal Court (ICC) statutes of 1998 as an act 'committed as part of a widespread or systematic attack directed against any civilian population, with knowledge of the attack'.

3. War crimes

Terrorist acts, if committed during military aggression, war or occupation, clearly also possess all the characteristics of war crimes, which are condemned by the four Geneva Conventions, the Hague convention of 1907, the Universal Declaration of Human Rights, and the UN Charter. Article 8 of the ICC statute on war crimes defines such crimes as grave violations against persons and property protected by the terms of the Geneva Conventions, which govern during an occupation.

The following are articles of the Geneva Conventions describing and condemning war crimes:

- Article 147 of the fourth Geneva Convention of 1949 states that the grave breaches noted in article 146, relative to the protection of civilian persons in time of war, include:
    - Wilful killing, torture or inhuman treatment, including biological experiments, wilfully causing great suffering or serious injury to body or health.
    - Compelling a protected person to serve in the forces of a hostile power.
    - Wilfully depriving a protected person of the rights of fair and regular trial prescribed in the present convention.
    - Taking of hostages and extensive destruction and appropriation of property not justified by military necessity and carried out unlawfully and wantonly.
- Article 3, also from the fourth Geneva Convention, states that, in the case of armed conflict not of an international character occurring in the territory of one of the higher contracting parties to the treaty, the following acts are and shall remain prohibited at any time and in any place whatsoever:
    - Violence to life and person, in particular murder of all kinds, mutilation, cruel treatment and torture.
    - Taking of hostages.

  - Outrages upon personal dignity, in particular humiliating and degrading treatment.
  - The passing of sentences and the carrying out of executions without previous judgement pronounced by a regularly constituted court, affording all the judicial guarantees which are recognised as indispensable by civilised people.

- As regards hostage taking, which is considered a war crime, it is firmly condemned by the following UN resolutions:
  - General Assembly resolution 44/29 'firmly calls for the immediate and safe release of all hostages and abducted persons, wherever and by whomever they are being held'.
  - UN Security Council resolution 687 of 3 April 1991, in which the Security Council for the first time made reference to the International Convention Against the Taking of Hostages, which categorises all acts of hostage-taking as 'manifestations of international terrorism'.
  - General Assembly resolution 46/51, 'measures to eliminate international terrorism', of 9 December 1991calls upon 'all states to use their political influence in accordance with the Charter of the United Nations and the principles of international law to secure the safe release of all hostages and abducted persons and to prevent the commission of acts of hostage-taking and abduction'.

4. Genocide

In 1948, the General Assembly of the United Nations passed an act called the International Convention on the Prevention and Punishment of the Crime of Genocide, also known as the Genocide Convention. This act, which took effect in 1951, provided a legal definition of genocide and established genocide as a crime under international law. According to the Genocide Convention, any of the following actions, when committed with the intent to eliminate a particular national, ethnic, racial, or religious group, constitutes genocide:

- Killing members of the group.

- Causing serious bodily or mental harm to members of the group.
- Deliberately inflicting on the group conditions of life calculated to kill.
- Imposing measures intended to prevent births within the groups.
- Forcibly transferring children out of a group.

Following the Nuremberg tribunal, individuals, especially high-ranking state officials and military commanders, have become accountable under international law for crimes committed by their military forces, which are not solely the responsibility of their state. Indeed, the Nuremberg tribunal declared that crimes against international peace and security and crimes against humanity are perpetrated by persons, not states.

5. The use and abuse of the word 'terrorism': 'self-defence' as a cover for state terrorism

Perhaps no other word has been more misused in contemporary politics as the word 'terrorism'; states have frequently thrown accusations of terrorism at each other, describing their enemies' activities as terrorism, and justifying their own violence and terrorism as 'self-defence', another word that has been extensively abused, together with terms like 'security', 'law and order', or even the 'war on terrorism', as an excuse to quell 'terroristic' activity.

The problem is that states, both democratic and undemocratic, tend to brand their political opponents — whether on the domestic or foreign level — as 'terrorists' in order to avoid any political dialogue and as a justification to crush any dissent.

Domestic terrorism that is perpetrated by the state against its own citizens or minorities, such as Saddam Hussein's gassing of Kurds and attacks against Shi'ites, or Milošević's systematic campaign of ethnic cleansing against Bosnians and ethnic Albanians, is no longer morally acceptable today with the prevalence of international humanitarian law over state sovereignty.

The only notable — and shameful - exception to this international outrage at the policy of state terrorism is Israel's unabashed policy of state terrorism, under the cover of 'self-defence', against Palestinian 'terrorists', a policy that is still allowed to continue unpunished.

Hence the need to provide evidentiary proof of the actual — instead of alleged — terroristic activity of a group, in order to avoid politically-motivated abuse of the word as a justification for state terrorism under the banner of 'fighting terrorism'.

6. State-sponsored terrorism: state terrorism's global reach

State terrorism often extends beyond the borders of a country to encompass the territory of neighbouring or even distant countries through direct aggression, invasion, or occupation, or indirectly by sponsoring terrorist or insurgent groups in these countries. State terrorism thus has a global reach and can take the form of financing, equipping, and training terrorist groups to carry out acts of violence against rival states.

Examples of such state-sponsored terrorism abound in contemporary world politics, being practised by 'democratic' as well as undemocratic states, whether directly or indirectly, tacitly or explicitly. State-sponsored terrorism is thus but another aspect of state terrorism and should be equally condemned with the same firmness and determination.

Consequences of state terrorism

State terrorism breeds international terrorism

International law tends to treat state terrorism and international terrorism as two distinct phenomena. Yet a close scrutiny shows that the main reasons international terrorism occurs is because of the oppressive and violent activities of states against their own minorities or the entire population, or against neighbouring countries through military repression, aggression, or occupation.

State terrorism often makes revolutionary terrorism — whether domestic or international in scope — inevitable, when state authorities use methods of terror and deny some or all of their citizens, or the population under occupation, their basic human rights and their right to self-determination, and crush any form of non-violent resistance.

If war is described as diplomacy by other means, then terrorism means war by unconventional means: the poor or the weak man's war, the last resort, the desperate weapon of a person who might otherwise be willing but unable to wage a conventional war against his more powerful foe. Therefore, although terrorism in all its forms should be condemned outright as an inhuman practice, it is often a consequence, not a cause, of violence and oppression; thus, in order to eradicate this scourge, we should treat the causes behind it, not only the symptoms, i.e. we should address the problem itself, which more often than not is state terrorism.

Examples of revolutionary organisations or guerrilla movements (which are in fact national liberation movements) that embody this despair among subjugated peoples are numerous: the PLO, the IRA, the ETA, the Kurdistan Workers' Party (PKK), Hezbollah, Hamas, the Armenian Secret Army for the Liberation of Armenia (ASALA), the Tamil Tigers, and so on. Based on the above, it becomes clear that hunting down terrorists with weapons alone will not solve the problem completely (on the contrary, it perpetuates it) so long as the anger among the oppressed still exists.

In this context, the UN General Assembly resolution 42/159 of 7 December 1987, on 'measures to prevent international terrorism which endangers or takes innocent human lives or jeopardises fundamental freedoms and study of the underlying causes of those forms of terrorism and acts of violence which lie in misery, frustration, grievance and despair and which cause some people to sacrifice human lives, including their own, in an attempt to effect radical changes', though deploring any taking of 'innocent human lives', does acknowledge that the causes of terrorism often lie in 'misery, frustration, grievance, and despair' that lead people to seek radical change by any means.

The said resolution also urges all states, unilaterally and in cooperation with other states, as well as relevant United Nations organs, to 'contribute to the progressive elimination of the causes underlying international terrorism and to pay special attention to all situations, including colonialism, racism and situations involving mass and flagrant violations of human rights and fundamental freedoms and those involving alien domination and occupation, that may give rise to international terrorism and may endanger international peace and security'.

This resolution establishes a clear and direct link between occupation, colonialism, and racism on the one hand, and international terrorism on the other hand.

Thus, in order to eliminate the endemic and chronic problem of terrorism in a permanent and consistent manner, its motives should be ended, motives that often lie in the misery and the frustration felt by oppressed, occupied, or colonised peoples. Hence, in order to end international terrorism, state terrorism should first be eliminated, for it is the breeding ground for international terrorism.

A quick glance at the list of foreign 'terrorist' organisations, with the notable exception of Islamist groups like al-Qaeda and its surrogates, reveals that most of these organisations, although they use methods of terror to achieve their objectives, have legitimate national aspirations and political demands and are fighting to end either oppression or occupation of their land, or struggling to achieve national self-determination. The method might be terroristic, yet the motive is legitimate.

Identifying the terrorists: a UN list of individuals, groups, and states practising terrorism

In order to ensure that the definition of terrorism covers all forms of terrorism, including state terrorism, and therefore to guarantee a universal jurisdiction for international law, and to avoid double standards and prevent the political abuse of the word terrorism in the war against terrorism, a comprehensive list of individuals, groups, and states practising or sponsoring terrorism should be set up under the UN's sole authority and supervision.

III

National Resistance versus Terrorism

The legitimacy of the struggle for self-determination and resistance to foreign occupation under international law

Much has been said about the need to distinguish between terrorism and legitimate resistance, but no clear attempt has been made to formulate this difference in legal terms rather than mere rhetoric. This distinction should not be hard to draw since international law clearly differentiates terrorism from legitimate national resistance to foreign military occupation, two radically opposed concepts which are linked only by opportunistic political manipulators who are opposed to certain groups which are fighting to achieve national self-determination.

International law recognises the right to resistance, the right of national resistance, in two cases:

1. In case resistance is used as a tool to exercise the right to self-determination

International law has been keen to affirm the right of peoples to determine, in a sovereign and independent manner free from any outside interference, the political, economic, and social order that they desire. Therefore, all states are legally bound under international law to respect the right of peoples to self-determination and to refrain from taking any measures or repressive acts which aim to deprive people of their right to sovereignty, freedom, and independence.

In case a civilian population is deprived of this right by coercive means such as occupation or repression, it has the full legitimate right, in accordance with the principles of the United Nations, to undertake to resist this repressive act by all available means, including national armed resistance, in order to recover this right and achieve self-determination; furthermore, it is legally allowed to receive outside assistance in its endeavour to restore its lost sovereignty or to realise its national aspirations.

The Charter of the United Nations has affirmed in a number of clauses the need to respect and uphold the right of peoples to self-determination without any impediment or reserve, and has prohibited member states from violating this right for any reason, urging them to refrain from the threat or use of force against the territorial integrity or political independence of any state, and sanctioning the cancellation of any international agreement that breaches or does not implement this right.

Thus, the inalienable right to self-determination and independence of all peoples is a pillar of international law, a principle that is as central to the UN Charter as the principle of state sovereignty.

In addition to the UN Charter, the following UN resolutions uphold the right of peoples to self-determination:

- UN General Assembly resolution 39/159, which reaffirms 'the inalienable right of all peoples to determine their own form of government and to choose their own economic, political and social system free from outside intervention, subversion, coercion and constraint of any kind whatsoever', and 'urges all States to respect and strictly observe, in accordance with the Charter of the United Nations, the sovereignty and political independence of States and the right of peoples to self-determination, as well as their right freely, without outside interference and intervention, to choose their socio-political system and to pursue their political, economic, social and cultural development'.

- UN General Assembly resolution 42/159, which condemns international terrorism, also reaffirms 'the principle of the self-determination of peoples as enshrined in the Charter of the United Nations', and the legitimacy of the national liberation movements of 'peoples under colonial and racist regimes and other forms of alien domination', concluding that nothing in the resolution should be taken to deny 'the right to self-determination, freedom, and independence of peoples.'

- UN General Assembly resolution 44/29, which reaffirms 'the principle of self-determination of peoples as enshrined in the Charter of the United Nations,' makes reference to the 'inalienable right to self-determination and independence of all peoples under colonial and racist regimes and other forms of alien domination and foreign occupation,' and upholds 'the legitimacy of their struggle, in particular the struggle of national liberation movements.'

Based on the above, any community or group struggling to achieve self-determination is legitimate in the eyes of international law. The Palestinians are a typical example of a community fighting to attain self-determination and to fulfil its national aspirations. Israel occupies land conquered in war in violation of international law; that is colonialism pure and simple. The struggle of the Palestinians is as legitimate as, say, the American War of Independence and the French Revolution. Failing to recognise the same right for the Palestinians is tantamount to dismissing all other struggles for freedom or wars of independence as terrorism.

2. In case resistance is used to end illegal foreign occupation

Occupation is illegitimate under international law

As mentioned earlier, military occupation by a foreign power is the highest form of state terrorism, and is condemned by international law. Occupation is indeed clearly considered illegal by international conventions and by the UN Charter, which states that 'all members shall refrain in their international relations from the threat or use of force against the territorial integrity or political independence of any state, or in any other manner inconsistent with the Purposes of the United Nations.'

General Assembly resolution 39/159 condemns state terrorism and also firmly denounces occupation as an illegitimate practice.

It also demands the renunciation of 'the threat or use of force against the territorial integrity or political independence of any State, non-intervention and non-interference in the internal and external affairs of States', and, upholding the 'permanent sovereignty of States and peoples over their natural resources, self-determination and independence of peoples under colonial domination, foreign occupation or racist regimes', demands that 'all States take no actions aimed at military intervention and occupation, forcible change in or undermining of the socio-political system of States, destabilisation and overthrow of their Governments and, in particular, initiate no military action to that end under any pretext whatsoever and cease forthwith any such action already in progress'.

To reiterate, the resolution also urges all states to respect and strictly observe, in accordance with the Charter of the United Nations, 'the sovereignty and political independence of States and the right of peoples to self-determination. There can be no clearer condemnation of occupation by international law.

Resisting occupation is sanctioned by international law

As foreign military occupation is viewed as illegal under international law, it follows that resisting this occupation is a legitimate act, for this resistance is aimed at ending the highest form of terrorism, which is state terrorism. National resistance became a legitimate right under international law following the occupations carried out by the Italian Fascists and the German Nazis in the Second World War. Nevertheless, people resisting occupation are branded 'terrorists' by other states, most especially, of course, by the occupying state.

Thus it was that the resistance fighters in the various occupied countries during the Second World War were viewed and treated as terrorists by Nazi Germany, while they were considered heroes by the Allies. Today, freedom fighters across the globe, who are considered 'terrorists' by many developed and developing countries, are treated as heroes by their peoples. However, this complete double standard, which is politically motivated, does not change the fact that national resistance to foreign military occupation is sanctioned by international law and all international conventions.

Hence the adage 'one man's terrorist is another man's freedom fighter' loses its meaning here, for all freedom fighters resisting foreign occupation are just that: freedom fighters; they are not 'terrorists', even as the fighters of the French Resistance in the Second World War were not 'terrorists'.

What applies to some should apply to all when it comes to labelling individuals or groups as either terrorists or freedom fighters; that is, if international law is to retain its legitimacy and restore its credibility in the eyes of the world. To consider Palestinian children who throw stones at Israeli occupation forces as 'terrorists', and to view the Israeli soldiers who return fire with live ammunition and shoot to kill as acting in self-defence, is a gross misrepresentation of the facts and a cynical and distorted view of events.

Resistance to occupation is sanctioned by international law, which stipulates that all means, including armed struggle, are legitimate to end an occupation, and that every assistance should be given to the freedom fighters by states toward this end. For its part the UN is obliged to apply Chapter Seven of the UN Charter to the occupying state; specifically, punitive measures ranging from economic sanctions to military action aimed at ending its invasion.

In this context, the UN Charter calls on all members to 'give the United Nations every assistance in any action it takes in accordance with the present Charter, and shall refrain from giving assistance to any state against which the United Nations is taking preventive or enforcement action'.

The following UN resolutions clearly support the legitimacy of national resistance:

- UN General Assembly resolution 42/159 includes a section that reaffirms the legitimacy of the national liberation movements, and 'considers that nothing in the present resolution could in any way prejudice the right to self-determination, freedom and independence, as derived from the Charter of the United Nations, of peoples forcibly deprived of that right, particularly peoples under colonial and racist regimes and foreign occupation or other forms of colonial domination, nor, in accordance with the principles of the Charter and in conformity with the above-mentioned Declaration, the right of theses peoples to struggle to this end and to seek and receive support'.

- UN General Assembly resolution 44/29, which upholds 'the legitimacy of their struggle, in particular the struggle of national liberation movements'.

From all of this, one can infer that:

a. Occupation is condemned by international law as an illegal practice.

b. The occupying force is bound by the principles of international humanitarian law, in particular the Fourth Geneva Convention pertaining to the protection of civilians under occupation. These duties are clear and specified and cover the civilians' persons, their property, their families, and their other human rights. In the event that the occupying country does not meet these duties or respect these rights, the civilian population is entitled to revolt against it by any necessary means, ranging from non-violent opposition to civil disobedience to armed struggle, until the occupation ends, and the said population is allowed to seek and to receive any assistance in its resistance against occupation.

   Indeed, despite international law's insistence that public order must be preserved even in occupied territories, it also aims to protect the right of peoples to self-determination when a certain population or group chooses to take up arms to liberate its land.

c. The use of force in order to resist occupation is thus sanctioned by international law, even though civilians who choose to take up arms lose their status of Protected Persons under the Fourth Geneva Convention.

d. Although resistance fighters are no longer considered civilians and lose their status as protected persons, they nevertheless retain their full human rights under the Geneva Conventions, which applies in time of war.

e. Any opposition or hindrance to a national liberation movement is considered unlawful under international law, whereas assisting this movement by all available means, such as funds, arms, equipment, training, and so forth is considered legitimate.

f. Annexation of occupied land conquered during war by the occupying force is considered illegitimate and hence is null and void under international law, and the resistance of the population under occupation to such an annexation is a legitimate right.

Hence, international law insists on the necessity of respecting the territorial integrity and unity of all states and their right to independence and sovereignty. Therefore, it is safe to conclude, based on what has been advanced, that Israel's occupation and partial annexation of the lands it conquered in 1967 is a flagrant violation of all international conventions, particularly the UN resolutions condemning this occupation, namely Security Council resolutions 242 and 338, which urge the Jewish entity to end its illegal occupation of Arab territories.

Since Israel has refused to abide by these resolutions, Palestinian resistance to its occupation is thus a legitimate right. Another typical example of Israel's unlawful actions is the latter's occupation of South Lebanon for more than two decades, and its continuing occupation of the Lebanese Shebaa farms. The Lebanese national resistance's operations against the Israeli occupation forces were thus considered legitimate under international law, and will remain lawful so long as the totality of Lebanese territory has not been liberated.

IV

Proposal for a Universal Definition of Terrorism

Based on the aforementioned criteria and conditions for a consensual definition of terrorism, the following is a proposal for a permanent, universal, and comprehensive definition of terrorism, to be adopted by the world community in an international conference on terrorism, which should be convened under the banner of the United Nations:

1. What is terrorism?

The term 'terrorism' means any unlawful use of force or any criminal acts of violence or threat thereof, wherever and by whomever they are committed, for whatever reason or justification, whether in an offensive, defensive or retaliatory manner, deliberately targeting the life, freedom and/or property of civilians who are not directly engaged in any unlawful or hostile activity — such as living on land or property that is confiscated, occupied or annexed by a foreign power — and aimed at spreading terror among the public, in furtherance of political objectives.

2. Acts of terrorism

Terrorist acts violate basic human rights and the humanitarian principles set forth in the UN Charter and the Universal Declaration of Human Rights, and thus fall under the category of — and should therefore be considered — crimes against humanity, war crimes, or crimes of genocide, in the form of wilful killing, assassination, mutilation, torture or inhuman treatment, hostage-taking, hijacking, aggression, illegal occupation, confiscation or annexation of land or property, damage to national resources or the environment or other public or private property, forced displacement or deportation of civilians, house demolitions, illegal settlements, detainment of people without trial, outrages upon personal dignity (in particular humiliating and degrading treatment), and incitement to genocide.

3. Forms and scope of terrorism

Terrorism has various forms and dimensions. It can be practised or sponsored by individuals, groups, or states, having a local, regional, or international scope.

Domestic terrorism: involves acts of terror that are confined to the boundaries of a state. Domestic terrorism falls into two categories:

a. Terrorism which is practised by individuals or sub- national groups, whether acting independently or sponsored by (a) foreign state(s), against the citizens and government officials and institutions of another state.

b. State terrorism, i.e. the unlawful use of violence or repression perpetrated by a state in the form of acts of terrorism mentioned in the second clause of the present definition, against some or all of its citizens, based on political, social, racial, religious, or cultural discrimination, or against the citizens of a territory occupied or annexed by the said state.

Regional or international terrorism: includes acts of terror involving countries of a certain region or across the globe, and committed by:

a. individuals or supra-national groups, acting independently or sponsored by (a) foreign state(s), or

b. states perpetrating or supporting acts of violence against the territory and citizens of other countries through direct aggression, invasion or occupation, or indirectly by sponsoring terrorist groups in these countries.

4. State terrorism as the highest form of terrorism

State terrorism, whether in its domestic or international dimensions (i.e. state-sponsored terrorism), is a flagrant violation of international law, namely UN General Assembly resolution 39/159, which firmly condemns such a policy, and constitutes the highest form of terrorism, given the fact that its violence and destruction are organised and practised by state authorities and agents and are thus sanctioned or condoned by the state's law, being viewed as legitimate by the government, whereas individual or group terrorism is practised by clandestine, outlaw groups whose members are fugitives wanted by both state and international law.

Therefore, states are urged not to employ unilaterally or abuse the word 'terrorism' to describe their opponents and thereby practise state terrorism under the fallacious label of 'self-defence', the United Nations being the sole authority that is qualified to define terrorism.

5. Occupation as a form of state terrorism

The invasion and illegal occupation of territories by a state are considered forms of state terrorism, for they constitute aggressive acts firmly condemned by international law as well as threats to international peace and security.

In this context, UN General Assembly resolution 39/159 condemns the policy of state terrorism, clearly describing occupation as a form of state terrorism. Foreign occupation and/or annexation of land is an unlawful act which blatantly violates the territorial integrity and sovereign independence — a principle that is a pillar of international law — of the occupied state, and strips its citizens of their freedom and their right to protection and security.

6. State terrorism breeds international terrorism

State terrorism frequently leads to international terrorism, when oppressive and unbearable measures are taken by state authorities against their own citizens or minorities. International terrorism is often itself not a cause but a consequence of violence and oppression.

Indeed, UN General Assembly resolution 42/159, established a clear and direct link between state terrorism and international terrorism, urging 'all states to contribute to the progressive elimination of the causes underlying international terrorism and to pay special attention to all situations, including colonialism, racism and situations involving mass and flagrant violations of human rights and fundamental freedoms and those involving alien domination and occupation, that may give rise to international terrorism and may endanger international peace and security'.

7. Resistance versus terrorism: The legitimacy of national resistance to foreign occupation under international law

Acts of armed national resistance to unlawful foreign military occupation, and against any entity that assists such acts, are legitimate under international law, namely UN General Assembly resolutions 39/159 and 42/159, which firmly prohibit such occupations, and are in full compliance with the international right of peoples to self-determination, which is a pillar of international law. These acts can therefore in no way whatsoever and under no circumstances be described as terrorist acts. Rather, resistance constitutes an outcome of foreign occupation that is condemned by all international conventions as a form of state terrorism, which has been established as a motive for terrorism.

8. The UN as the sole body for defining and fighting terrorism

In order to ensure the universality of the definition of terrorism, as well as to guarantee the global scope of the fight against terrorism, the present definition of terrorism should meet the general approval of the international community and thus be endorsed by the United Nations and the qualified majority of its member states, having a binding effect on all. To achieve this universality, the United Nations should be the sole authority and the only legal and political framework for any counter-terrorist resolutions or measures, or any international coalition against terrorism.

UN resolutions and recommendations concerning terrorism are therefore binding on all member states, which are urged to harmonise their domestic legislation with international conventions relating to terrorism. In this context, steps should be taken to empower and activate the International Criminal Court that was established in Rome in 1998 and which entered into force in 2002, in order to judge those accused of crimes against humanity, war crimes and acts of genocide, all of which are terrorist acts, wherever and by whomever committed.

The ICC, whose prerogatives cover the trial of war criminals and perpetrators of crimes against humanity, should work in concert with the International Court of Justice (ICJ).

An international conference on terrorism should thus take place under the banner of the United Nations and in accordance with UN General Assembly resolution 44/29, to adopt or amend the present definition of terrorism, which should serve as a guideline for UN policy to achieve global justice.

This conference should also establish a list of individuals, groups, and states practising or sponsoring terrorism, as well as a list of resistance groups fighting against foreign occupation or to achieve national self-determination, in order to avoid any confusion in identifying these two antithetical groups, and to avoid any abuse of the word 'terrorism' as an excuse to practise arbitrary repression or violence under the guise of 'self-defence' or the 'war on terrorism'.

Any changes to the present definition of terrorism or to the aforementioned lists are to be made solely under UN supervision and pending the approval of a qualified majority of its member states.

Appendix I: State Terrorism – The Case of Israel

Israel is an outlaw state and a rogue state. Its very existence and practices are a flagrant violation of international law, which condemns the foreign occupation and annexation of land as well as state terrorism against citizens of an occupied or annexed land. The establishment of the State of 'Israel' in 1948 in the occupied parts of Palestine on the southern border of Lebanon, and Israel's subsequent policies towards Palestinians and its Arab neighbours since its creation, are entirely in conflict with the spirit and letter of the Universal Declaration of Human Rights.

The proclamation of the establishment of the State of Israel was a flagrant violation of the natural right of the Palestinian people to live on their land, and of their right to self-determination, to their own property and to live in dignity. Ever since its artificial creation and up to the present day, Israel has been practising state terrorism against Palestinians and against neighbouring states, Lebanon in particular, claiming the lives of tens of thousands of innocent victims, leaving untold destruction and impeding the economic, social and political development of the countries of the entire region.

The devastating effects of the establishment of the state of 'Israel' on the entire Middle East are still felt to this day, especially by Palestinians, who continue to live in abject and unacceptable conditions and suffer the humiliating and violent practices of an occupying force which shows blatant disregard for human rights, as well as by the Lebanese people who have suffered greatly and for long decades from Israel's state terrorism.

Indeed, Israeli policy towards Lebanon, over the past three decades in particular, has been one of sustained and devastating aggression and complete disregard for the sovereignty of this state and the rights of its inhabitants.

1. Israel's state terrorism against Lebanon from 1978 to 2006

Israel, which has been practising state terrorism against Lebanon since 1978 through both invasion and other forms of aggression, using all methods of terror against the Lebanese civilian population, has thereby violated all international conventions and several UN resolutions as well as the Universal Declaration of Human Rights and the Charter of the United Nations, committing all varieties of war crimes, crimes against humanity, and acts of genocide during its 22-year occupation of Lebanon and its renewed aggression against Lebanon in 2006. Additionally, Israel continues to this day to violate Lebanon's airspace on a daily basis.

Israel's major military attacks against Lebanon were the following:

- The invasion of March 1978
- The attack of July 1981
- The invasion of June 1982
- The attack of July 1993
- The attack of April 1996
- The invasion of July 2006

This dark period of Israeli occupation and aggression was characterised by many violations of the basic human rights to life, liberty, dignity and property, and by tragedies and disasters affecting the majority of families in Lebanon. Indeed, Israel's state terrorism has caused huge material losses estimated at tens of billions of US dollars, as well as the deaths of tens of thousands of Lebanese citizens and the injury of hundreds of thousands, with women, children, and elderly people accounting for most of those casualties. Israel's many aggressions also caused successive waves of displacement of hundreds of thousands of Lebanese civilians from scores of towns and villages.

Israel's terroristic practices also involved several massacres of civilians, most horrific among these being the Qana massacre of 1996, when Israeli warplanes deliberately targeted the UN compound at Qana in southern Lebanon, thus causing the deaths of 108 Lebanese civilians, mostly women, children, and elderly persons who had taken refuge from Israeli bombing.

In parallel to its occupation and the repeated acts of aggression that affected the lives of thousands of Lebanese families, Israel pursued a number of practices in the areas which it occupied that demonstrate utter contempt for the norms and principles agreed upon by the international community in its conventions. There were numerous instances of Israel's disregard for, in particular, the Geneva Convention relative to the Protection of Civilian Persons in Time of War (12 August 1949).

Among its many violations of human rights, Israel has also practised torture and other human rights abuses in its detention centres in southern Lebanon, where arbitrarily arrested Lebanese civilians were illegally detained without a fair trial or judgement, as Amnesty International and Red Cross reports testify, not to mention the Lebanese detainees still being held hostage in Israeli prisons to this day.

Despite the forced withdrawal of its occupation forces in 2000 due to the heroic Lebanese resistance operations, Israel launched another deadly and devastating war against Lebanon in 2006 and still persists in its violations of international law through its continued occupation of parts of Lebanese territory and the Shebaa farms, as well as its daily violations of Lebanese airspace.

Notable and typical examples of Israel's state terrorism are the two operations 'Accountability' (July 1993) and 'Grapes of Wrath' (April 1996), in which Israel's stated political objective was to spread terror and foment a refugee flow from southern Lebanon to the north in order to put pressure on the Lebanese government, so that it, in turn, would curb resistance actions by Hezbollah.

In a report on 'Operation Accountability', Human Rights Watch (HRW) asserts: 'While Israel has claimed that broadcast warnings to the civilian population in southern Lebanon were made with a view to protecting civilians from collateral injury in attacks on strictly military objectives, a number of factors make it reasonable to assume that the intention was in fact to sow terror among the civilian population'.

As the pattern of physical damage showed, the report continues, the Israel Defence Forces and its band of mercenaries, the 'South Lebanon Army' 'subjected entire villages to aerial bombardment. The threats and the nature of the attacks make it clear that in significant areas in southern Lebanon whole populations — indeed anyone who failed to flee by a certain time — were targeted as if they were combatants'.

HRW estimates that some 120 civilians were killed and close to 50 injured during the operation. In addition, the bombing led to the immediate displacement of an estimated 150,000 to 200,000 people. Less than three years later, Israel launched a similar attack, this time cynically calling it 'Grapes of Wrath'. According to Israel's daily *Haaretz* (21 April 1996), the military command of the northern borders' internal report indicates that, in the first few days of the operation, Israeli planes bombed 300 sites in Lebanon, resulting in the displacement of approximately 400,000 civilians and the demolition of over 200 houses.

Moreover, some 198 civilians were killed, including the 108 refugees in the village of Qana, which thus witnessed another macabre massacre like the one perpetrated in 1993. These operations are characteristic cases of terrorism pure and simple and correspond to all known definitions of terrorism, for they target the life, freedom, and property of civilians, they are ruthlessly destructive, and unpredictable as to who will be under attack, indiscriminately targeting military as well as civilian lives, and their aim is clearly to kill or spread terror among the civilian population.

Israeli practices and attacks against Lebanon and its citizens have repeatedly been harshly condemned by international organisations, and were regularly censured at the annual meetings in Geneva of the Commission on Human Rights.

Deliberate Israeli attacks on Lebanese civilians

During the 30 years of military operations carried out by Israeli forces against Lebanon, civilians have been consistently and directly targeted, the prime objective being to cause the greatest number of casualties among them in order to drive them off their land and subject them to the control of the military administration, as well as to annex territory.

This was all part of the standard policy, which consisted of causing deaths and injuries, practising intimidation and torture, imprisoning and expelling citizens, destroying crops, cutting down wild and fruit trees, blockading villages and so on. The arbitrary measures and encroachment to which these villages have been subjected included:

- Air raids against residential homes, resulting in massacres in which hundreds were killed and thousands injured.

- Daily shelling by different types of artillery, resulting in deaths and injuries to civilians and the destruction of their homes, their workplaces, their fields and their places of worship.
- Booby-trapped packages were dropped by Israeli planes targeting civilians, herdsmen and farmers, maiming or killing them as they travel to their homes or to work. Additionally, thousands of booby-trapped toys were dropped targeting children.
- Forced migration of peaceful inhabitants from their towns and villages. As a result of the recurrent invasions and attacks, hundreds of thousands of civilians were forced to become refugees.
- Arbitrary arrests were made, leading to imprisonment as well as mental and physical torture.
- Sieges of villages and townships whose inhabitants were unlawfully confined, and the delivery of humanitarian assistance was blocked.
- Houses belonging to the families of resistance fighters were blown up by the Israeli forces and their client militia, in violation of Article 17, paragraph 2 of the Universal Declaration of Human Rights, which stipulates that 'no one shall be arbitrarily deprived of property'.
- Ports were blockaded and fishermen prevented from fishing, which provides a livelihood for thousands of needy families. A number of fishermen were also arrested, beaten and tortured, and their boats and nets destroyed.
- Thousands of citizens were expelled from their villages and prevented from returning, in particular those who refused to cooperate with the Israeli occupying authorities, and by association, their families, in violation of Article 49 of the Fourth Geneva Convention.
- Lebanese have been prevented from harvesting their crops, orchards have been set alight and agricultural produce have been destroyed with phosphorous shells and other internationally prohibited weapons, forcing inhabitants to migrate.
- The establishment of a police state using members of the Israeli army and its client forces in the occupied border strip, which

curtailed all types of freedoms and paralysed political, economic, social and cultural life, and imposed compulsory conscription on the Lebanese youth belonging to the so-called 'South Lebanon Army', their client militia. Those who refused conscription were arrested, in violation of Article 51 of the Geneva Conventions.

- Ambulances belonging to the Lebanese Red Cross and other accredited organisations were deliberately targeted (as was particularly the case during the Israeli attacks of 1993 and 1996), as have hospitals, despite the fact that the Geneva Conventions clearly and categorically prohibit attacks on ambulances, hospitals and medical staff in general.
- Israel issued threats against the civilian population through its officials in the occupied areas. Such threats are contrary to Article 51, paragraph 2 of Protocol I of the Geneva Conventions, which prohibits acts or threats of violence when the primary purpose is to spread terror among the civilian population.
- Israel deliberately targeted the Lebanese infrastructure during its many assaults, particularly in 1996 when it deliberately bombed two power stations and 12 water facilities, and again in 2006 when it bombed several bridges and the fuel oil plant in Jiyeh, causing the worst environmental disaster in the region in which thousands of tons of heavy fuel oil were spilled into the Mediterranean.
- During its 22 years of brutal occupation, Israel left behind nearly 400,000 mines which continue to inflict casualties daily, killing hundreds of Lebanese civilians and wounding thousands.
- During the 2006 war, Israel dropped over 1.5 million cluster bombs — which are internationally prohibited weapons — on southern Lebanon, in heavily populated areas, bombs which – likewise continue to cause death and injury among the civilian population.

Israeli massacres of civilians in Lebanon 1948-2006

- Hula massacre, 1948: 90 civilians killed, mostly children, elderly, and disabled persons
- Hula massacre, 1967: five women killed
- Hanin massacre, 1967: 20 civilians killed
- Bin Jbeil massacre, 1976: 23 civilians killed, 30 wounded
- Uzai massacre, 1978: 36 civilians killed, others wounded
- Rashayya Adlun massacre, 1978: 15 civilians killed
- Adlun massacre, 1978: 17 civilians killed, 3 wounded
- Khiyam massacre, 1978: over 100 civilians killed, mostly elderly people aged between 70 and 85
- Abbasiyah massacre, 1978: 40 civilians killed, mostly women and children, hundreds of others wounded
- Kunin massacre, 1978: 16 civilians killed
- Sabra and Shatila massacre, 1982: 3,500 Palestinian refugees killed, including women, children, infants, and elderly
- Suhmur massacre, 1984: 13 civilians killed, 12 wounded
- Sir al-Gharbiyah massacre, 1985: 7 civilians killed, several others wounded
- Ma'rakah massacre, 1985: 15 civilians killed, 45 wounded
- Bir al-Abd massacre, 1985: 75 civilians killed, mostly women and children
- Zrariyah massacre, 1985: 22 civilians killed
- Al-Tuffah area massacre, 1985: 30 civilians killed, hundreds wounded
- Dayr al-Zahrani, 1994: 8 civilians killed, 17 others wounded.
- Suhmur massacre, 1996: 8 civilians killed
- Nabatiyah massacre, 1996: a woman and her seven children were killed

- Qana slaugher, 1996: 107 civilians killed, including 33 children
- Second Qana massacre, 2006: 28 civilians killed, including 16 children, and another 16 reported missing

Internationally proscribed weapons used by Israel in Lebanon since 1978

Since it first occupied Lebanese territory in 1978, Israel has used internationally proscribed weapons like white phosphorous and fragmentation bombs to shell populated villages and towns. It has done so in defiance of international agreements which specifically ban and provide sanctions against any state which uses these weapons, particularly against civilians.

In this connection, reference must be made to the 1899 Hague Declaration concerning the Prohibition of the Use of Expanding Bullets and the 1925 Geneva Protocol for the Prohibition of the Use in War of Asphyxiating, Poisonous or other Gases, and of Bacteriological Methods of Warfare.

Reference must also be made to resolution HR/CN/755 passed on 4 September 1996 by the UN Sub-commission on Prevention of Discrimination and Protection of Minorities, in which it condemned the use of depleted uranium (DU) and certain other weapons during its 48th session in September 1996. The sub-commission urged all states 'to be guided in their national policies by the need to curb production and spread of weapons of mass destruction or with indiscriminate effect, in particular nuclear weapons, chemical weapons, fuel-air bombs, napalm, cluster bombs, biological weaponry and weaponry containing depleted uranium'.

Israel's use of internationally proscribed weapons has caused serious material damage and severe injuries to their victims, inflicting permanent physical disabilities on many of them.

The primary types of internationally prohibited weapons used by the Israeli forces in Lebanon, mainly against civilians, are the following:

- Nail bombs
- Phosphorous bombs and bombs known as al-Tarmid and al-Tarasid

- Fragmentation bombs and missiles
- Cluster bombs (Tal 1)
- Israeli 120-mm cluster bomb (CL3144 ICM)

Human rights violations in Israeli detention camps in southern Lebanon

The Israeli occupation forces established a number of detention camps in the occupied part of southern Lebanon, and illegally detained hundreds of Lebanese citizens in these camps, including women, men of all ages, and boys. These camps were supervised by Israeli army officers. Contrary to international law and custom, the occupation forces transferred dozens of the detainees to prisons inside Israel and sentenced them to incarceration for terms ranging from 10 to 30 years, without any trial.

These detainees were in effect hostages who did not enjoy the protection for which provision is made in the Geneva Convention of 1949 on protection of civilians. Israel kept them in what it called 'administrative detention' for long periods of time, in clear violation of international law, since the detainee was given no opportunity to defend himself or to retain a lawyer, nor was he allowed to be interviewed. The International Committee of the Red Cross (ICRC) failed repeatedly to persuade the Israelis to allow its representatives to visit any of these detention camps, including the notorious Khiam camp and the other camps in the occupied border strip, to check on conditions there.

Israel tried to deceive the international community into believing that the Khiam camp and the other detention camps were administered by the collaborationist militia known as the 'South Lebanon Army', but Amnesty International found strong indications that Israeli intelligence officers were involved in the administration of the camps and in the interrogation and torture of detainees.

The actions of the Israeli occupation forces in apprehending and detaining dozens of Lebanese citizens, holding them unlawfully without trial, continuing to detain some of them after the completion of their sentences, and torturing them contravened the Hague and Geneva Conventions, especially articles 49 and 76 of the Third Geneva Convention. These measures also contravened the Universal

Declaration of Human Rights, which prohibits torture and the arbitrary deprivation of liberty and the right to a fair trial.

The preamble to the Declaration refers to the need to recognise 'the inherent dignity of all members of the human family' and 'the dignity of the human person'.

Article 5 of the Universal Declaration of Human Rights, for its part, states that 'no one shall be subjected to torture or to cruel, inhuman or degrading treatment or punishment'.

Article 9 of the Universal Declaration of Human Rights states that no one shall be subjected to arbitrary arrest, detention or exile. The same principle is reiterated in Article 9 of the International Covenant on Civil and Political Rights.

In violation of all these international agreements, the Israeli authorities deliberately tortured Lebanese and other detainees and subjected them to degrading treatment, both in the Khiam detention camp in the occupied border strip and in Israeli prisons.

Conditions in the Khiam and other detention camps were inhumane. Any form of misbehaviour was severely punished, over and above such collective punishments as refusing to provide the prisoners with water for washing, depriving them of food, and giving them only a small can for sanitary purposes in their sleeping quarters.

Health care was virtually nonexistent: illnesses were treated with aspirin and sedatives, and there were no periodic medical inspections to check up on the state of the inmates' health. Indeed, a number of injured inmates were deliberately left untreated as a form of torture.

The persons being held in Khiam detention camp were subjected to torture in many forms.

Physical torture:

Detainees were subjected to:

- The electric chair
- Electric shocks
- Beating with wire cables
- Hanging

  Some detainees were hung from a lighting fixture with their hands handcuffed over their heads and a concrete block was placed under their feet. The concrete block was then kicked away, and the detainees were left suspended and standing on tiptoe for approximately 30 hours

- Confinement in 'the hole', which is a cell measuring not more than 50 cm by 70 cm high and flooded with water
- Confinement in an unlit cell for long periods
- Deprivation of sleep, food and medical facilities
- Handcuffs and leg irons, with a bag placed over the head

Mental torture:

- Threats to have the individual's family incarcerated
- Solitary confinement
- Torture of close relatives
- Threats of the use of force

Women and girls were tortured by the same methods as were used on the men. In addition, they were stripped naked and beaten with cables on sensitive parts of their bodies during interrogation, and electrical shocks were administered to other sensitive areas such as the breasts, with a view to humiliating them, thus subjecting them to both physical and mental torture.

Israel also authorised pharmaceutical companies to perform hazardous medical experiments on detainees in the camps of the occupied zone, in a grave violation of human rights.

Amnesty International revealed the methods of torture used in Israeli prisons and demanded assurances that resort to those methods would cease, but to no avail.

2. Israel's state terrorism violates all international conventions

Israel's state terrorism, whether in the form of aggression, invasion, occupation, wilful killing, torture, and so on is in clear violation of all international conventions, particularly the UN Charter, the Universal

Declaration of Human Rights, and UN Security Council resolutions 242, 338, and 425, to name but a few. It likewise violates the Geneva Conventions of 1949 and the first additional protocol of 1977, the Hague Convention of 1907, and the UN General Assembly resolution of 1997 that condemns the colonialist policies of Israel in Jerusalem.

Israel's grave violations of UN resolutions and the Geneva Conventions

Israel's above-mentioned terrorist acts fall under the category of crimes against humanity, war crimes, and acts of genocide, and thus represent a clear breach of basic human rights as stipulated in the following articles of the Geneva Conventions and the statutes of the International Criminal Court:

- Article 7 of the ICC statutes of 1998, which describes a crime against humanity as an act 'committed as part of a widespread or systematic attack directed against any civilian population, with knowledge of the attack'.
- Article 8 of the ICC statute on war crimes that describes the latter as grave violations against persons and property protected by the terms of the Geneva Conventions, which govern during occupation.

In this context, the Sabra and Shatila massacres of Palestinian refugees, which were perpetrated during the aggressive invasion of the Israeli army into Lebanese territory in 1982, are a typical example of Israel's numerous war crimes. The Israeli army was, at the time, an occupation force in the sense of Article 4 of the Fourth Geneva Convention, and this army therefore had a clear responsibility towards the protected persons, in conformity with Article 146 of the Geneva Conventions relative to the protection of civilian persons in time of war. The victims of Sabra and Shatila were considered as Protected Persons as defined in the Fourth Geneva Convention, particularly Article 147.

Article 147 of the Geneva Conventions states that the grave breaches noted in Article 146, relative to the protection of civilian persons in time of war, include:

- Wilful killing, torture or inhuman treatment, including biological experiments, wilfully causing great suffering or serious injury to body or health
- Compelling a protected person to serve in the forces of a hostile power
- Wilfully depriving a protected person of the right to a fair and regular trial prescribed in the present convention
- Taking of hostages and extensive destruction and appropriation of property, not justified by military necessity and carried out unlawfully and wantonly

Article 3, which is common to the four Geneva Conventions of 1949, states that, in the case of armed conflict not of an international character occurring in the territory of one of the higher contracting parties, the following acts of violence are and shall remain prohibited at any time and in any place whatsoever:

- Violence to life and person, in particular murder of all kinds, mutilation, cruel treatment and torture
- Taking of hostages
- Outrages upon personal dignity, in particular humiliating and degrading treatment
- The passing of sentences and the carrying out of executions without previous judgement pronounced by a regularly constituted court, affording all the judicial guarantees which are recognised as indispensable by civilised people

As regards hostage taking, a practice extensively used by the Israeli occupation forces, it is firmly condemned by the following UN resolutions:

- General Assembly resolution 44/29, 'firmly calls for the immediate and safe release of all hostages and abducted persons, wherever and by whomever they are being held'.
- UN Security Council resolution 687, in which the Security Council for the first time made reference to the International Convention against the Taking of Hostages, which categorises

all acts of taking hostages as 'manifestations of international terrorism'.

- General Assembly resolution 46/51 calls upon 'all states to use their political influence in accordance with the Charter of the United Nations and the principles of international law to secure the safe release of all hostages and abducted persons and to prevent the commission of acts of hostage-taking and abduction'.

Israeli attacks against civilians and international law

By carrying out attacks against civilians in Lebanon, Israel has directly violated the right to life and the right to security of person, as provided for under Article 3 of the Universal Declaration of Human Rights and Article 6 of the International Covenant on Civil and Political Rights.

Israel has consistently flouted the norms and principles of international law which clearly and unequivocally prohibit direct and indiscriminate attacks against civilians. It repeatedly contravened Additional Protocol I to the Geneva Conventions of 1949, as well as the Protection of Victims of International Armed Conflicts, whose basic provisions, particularly those relating to civilian populations, constitute an integral part of the norms of international law by which all states are bound.

By attacking civilians on Lebanese territory, Israel has violated the following articles of the first protocol to the Geneva Conventions of 1949:

a. Prohibition of direct attacks against the civilian population (referred to as the 'basic rule' of the principle of distinction):

Article 48, which provides as follows:

> 'In order to ensure respect for and protection of the civilian population and civilian objects, the Parties to the conflict shall at all times distinguish between the civilian population and combatants and between civilian objects and military objectives and accordingly shall direct their operations only against military objects.'

Article 51 (2), which provides as follows:

'The civilian population as such, as well as individual civilians, shall not be the object of attack.'

b. Prohibition of indiscriminate attacks:

Article 51 (4), which provides as follows:

'Indiscriminate attacks are prohibited. Indiscriminate attacks are:

- Those which are not directed at a specific military objective;
- Those which employ a method or means of combat which cannot be directed at a specific military objective; or
- Those which employ a method or means of combat the effects of which cannot be limited as required by this Protocol; and consequently, in each such case, are of a nature to strike military objectives and civilians or civilian objects without distinction.'

The Israeli armed forces carried out indiscriminate attacks in contravention of the principle of distinction, attacking military targets at random and without regard for their effect upon the civilian population and using fragmentation weapons or weapons that are not equipped for target discrimination. The regular use of this tactic demonstrated a blatant disregard for civilian lives and property.

There is plenty of evidence to show that Israel carried out indiscriminate attacks against Lebanese civilians. In one of the most horrific incidents, during the so-called 'Operation Grapes of Wrath' in 1996, Israel was responsible for a massacre at Qana in which it shelled the battalion headquarters of the Fijian contingent of the United Nations Interim Force in Lebanon (UNIFIL), killing over one hundred civilians. In statements to the local and international media, Israel alleged that the base was being used by 'enemy forces', which of course is totally untrue.

According to Article 51 of the first additional protocol to the Geneva Conventions of 1949, an indiscriminate attack is: 'An attack by bombardment by any methods or means which treats as a single military objective a number of clearly separated and distinct military objectives located in a city, town, village or other are containing a similar concentration of civilians or civilian objects.'

Israel's breaches of the Genocide Convention

During its numerous military aggressions, Israel has frequently committed crimes of genocide against Lebanese and Palestinian civilians, and continues to practice many of the following criminal acts against Palestinians in the Occupied Territories, any of which, according to the Genocide Convention, constitutes genocide, when committed with the intent of eliminating members of a national, ethnic, racial or religious group:

- Killing members of the group
- Causing serious bodily or mental harm to members of the group
- Deliberately inflicting on the group conditions of life calculated to kill
- Imposing measures intended to prevent births within the groups
- Forcibly transferring children out of a group

The massacres perpetrated at the Sabra and Shatila Palestinian refugee camps constitute a crime of genocide, as confirmed by the United Nations General Assembly Resolution 37/123D which considers this massacre as an act of genocide, as well as a crime against humanity, a war crime and a grave violation of the Geneva Conventions.

Israeli leaders and military commanders are responsible under international law for any crimes committed by their military forces. They are not solely the responsibility of their state. Indeed, the Nuremberg tribunal declared that crimes against international peace and security and crimes against humanity are perpetrated by persons, not states, and therefore these persons should be held accountable and tried in an international criminal court, the same way that Slobodan Milošević was brought to trial.

UN Security Council resolutions condemning Israeli state terrorism and Israeli violations of UN Resolutions

The following is a list of United Nations Security Council resolutions directly condemning Israel for the state terrorism that the Zionist entity has been practising since its creation, namely its violations of UN Security Council resolutions, the UN Charter, the Geneva Conventions, and other violations of international law:

- Resolution 57 dated 18 September 1948, in which the Security Council expressed its profound shock at the assassination of the United Nations mediator in Palestine, Count Bernadotte, in a cowardly act by a group of Zionist terrorists in Jerusalem.
- Resolution 59 dated 19 October 1948, in which the Security Council expressed its concern over the fact of Israel's not having submitted a report on the assassination of Count Bernadotte, and proclaiming it to be the duty of governments throughout the world to cooperate with the supervisory body.
- Resolution 60 dated 29 October 1948, in which the Security Council resolved to establish a sub-committee to revise the draft resolution with regard to the situation in Jerusalem.
- Resolution 61 dated 4 November 1948, in which the Security Council called for the withdrawal of Israeli forces and the establishment of permanent truce lines.
- Resolution 89 dated 17 November 1950, in which the Security Council requested that attention be given to the expulsion of 'thousands of Palestine Arabs' and called upon concerned governments to take no further action 'involving the transfer of persons across international frontiers or armistice lines', and noted that Israel announced that it would withdraw to the armistice lines.
- Resolution 92 dated 8 May 1951, in which the Security Council asked for a ceasefire in the demilitarised zone along the Syrian-Israeli truce lines.
- Resolution 93 dated 18 May 1951, in which the Security Council considered that Israeli airstrikes on Syria on 5 April 1951 constitute 'a violation of the cease-fire', and decided that

Arab civilians expelled from the demilitarised zone by Israel should be allowed to return.

- Resolution 100 dated 27 October 1953, in which the Security Council asked Israel to cease water drainage and rerouting operations in the demilitarised zone from Hawlah.
- Resolution 101 dated 24 November 1953, in which the Security Council condemned the Israeli attack on Qubiya of 14-15 October 1953, the Council having found that the retaliatory Israeli action against Qubiya and all similar acts represent violations of the ceasefire agreement issued in Security Council Resolution No. 54 of 1948, and 'expresses the strongest censure of that action'.
- Resolution 106 dated 29 March 1955, in which the Security Council condemned Israel's attack on Egyptian forces in the Gaza Strip on 28 February 1955, having judged such aggression to be a premeditated attack on the part of Israeli authorities carried out by the Israeli standing army against the Egyptian standing army in the Gaza Strip.
- Resolution 111 dated 19 January 1956, in which the Security Council condemned the Israeli aggression against Syria on 11 December 1955 (the Lake Tiberius region) as 'a flagrant violation of the cease-fire' and armistice agreement, the Israeli standing army having carried out an attack on the Syrian standing army forces on Syrian territory.
- Resolution 119 dated 31 October 1956, in which the Security Council considers that 'a grave situation has been created'by the attack against Egypt by the forces of Britain, France, and Israel.
- Resolution 171 dated 9 April 1962, in which the Security Council 'determines flagrant violations [of Resolution 111] by Israel in its attack on Syria' on 16 March 1962.
- Resolution 228 dated 25 November 1966, in which the Security Council 'deplores the loss of life and heavy damage to property resulting from the action' by Israel in the southern Hebron area on 13 November 1966, and 'censures Israel for this large-scale

military action in violation of the United Nations Charter' and the armistice agreement between Israel and Jordan.

- Resolution 233 dated 6 June 1967, Six Day War.
- Resolution 234 dated 7 June 1967, Six Day War.
- Resolution 235 dated 9 June 1967, Six Day War.
- Resolution 236 dated 11 June 1967, Six Day War.
- Resolution 237 dated 14 June 1967, Six Day War, in which the Security Council called on Israel 'to ensure the safety, welfare and security of the inhabitants where military operations have taken place' during the war launched by Israel on 5 June 1967 'and to facilitate the return of those inhabitants who have fled the areas since the outbreak of hostilities'.
- Resolution 240 dated 25 October 1967, Six Day War, concerning violations of the ceasefire.
- Resolution 242 dated 22 November 1967, in which the Security Council emphasised 'the inadmissibility of the acquisition of territory by war', and further emphasised that member states have a commitment to abide by the UN Charter, and called for the 'withdrawal of Israeli armed forces from territories occupied' during the June 1967 war. It is commonly interpreted today as calling for the 'land for peace' principle as a way to resolve the Arab-Israeli conflict.
- Resolution 248 dated 24 March 1968, in which the Security Council observed that the Israeli attack on Jordan 'was of a large-scale and carefully planned nature', 'deplores the loss of life and heavy damage to property', 'condemns the military action launched by Israel in flagrant violation of the United Nations Charter and the cease-fire resolutions', and 'calls upon Israel to desist from' further violations of Resolution 237.
- Resolution 250 dated 27 April 1968, in which the Security Council considered 'that the holding of a military parade in Jerusalem will aggravate tensions in the area and have an adverse effect on a peaceful settlement of the problems in the area' and 'calls upon Israel to refrain from holding the military parade in Jerusalem which is contemplated' for 2 May 1968.

- Resolution 251 dated 2 May 1968, in which the Security Council recalled Resolution 250 and 'deeply deplores the holding by Israel of the military parade in Jerusalem' on 2 May 1968 'in disregard of' Resolution 250.
- Resolution 252 dated 21 May 1968 in which the Security Council 'deplores the failure of Israel to comply with' General Assembly resolutions 2253 and 2254, considered Israel's annexation of Jerusalem 'invalid', and called upon Israel 'to rescind all such measures already taken and to desist forthwith from taking any further action which tends to change the status of Jerusalem'.
- Resolution 256 dated 16 August 1968, in which the Security Council condemned Israeli military raids on Jordan as 'flagrant violations', recalled Israel's 'flagrant violation of the United Nations Charter' condemned in Resolution 248, observed that further Israeli air attacks on Jordan 'were of a large scale and carefully planned nature in violation of resolution 248', 'deplores the loss of life and heavy damage to property', and condemned Israel's attacks.
- Resolution 258 dated 18 September 1968, in which the Security Council expressed 'concern' with the welfare of the inhabitants of the Israeli-occupied territories, and requests a special representative to be sent to report on the implementation of Resolution 237, and that Israel cooperate.
- Resolution 259 dated 27 September 1968, in which the Security Council expressed concern for 'the safety, welfare and security' of the Palestinians 'under military occupation by Israel', deplored 'the delay in the implementation of Resolution 237 (1967) because of the conditions still being set by Israel for receiving a Special Representative of the Secretary-General', and requested Israel to receive the Special Representative and facilitate his work.
- Resolution 262 dated 31 December 1968, in which the Security Council observed 'that the military action by the armed forces of Israel against the civil International Airport of Beirut was

premeditated and of a large scale and carefully planned nature', and condemns Israel for the attack.

- Resolution 265 dated 1 April 1969, in which the Security Council expressed 'deep concern that the recent attacks on Jordanian villages and other populated areas were of a pre-planned nature, in violation of resolutions [248 and 256]deplores the loss of civilian life and damage to property', and 'condemns the recent premeditated air attacks launched by Israel on Jordanian villages and populated areas in flagrant violation of the United Nations Charter and the cease-fire resolutions'.
- Resolution 267 dated 3 July 1969, in which the Security Council censured Israel for administrative acts changing the status of Jerusalem, recalled resolution 252 and General Assembly resolutions 2253 and 2254, and noted that 'since the adoption of the above-mentioned resolutions Israel has taken further measures tending to change the status of the City of Jerusalem', reaffirmed 'the established principle that acquisition of territory by military conquest is inadmissible', 'deplores the failure of Israel to show any regard for the resolutions', 'censures in the strongest terms all measures taken to change the status of the City of Jerusalem', 'confirms that all legislative and administrative measures and actions taken by Israel which purport to alter the status of Jerusalem, including expropriation of land and properties thereon, are invalid and cannot change that status', and urgently called on Israel to rescind the measures taken to annex Jerusalem.
- Resolution 270 dated 26 August 1969, in which the Security Council 'condemns the premeditated air attack by Israel on villages in southern Lebanon in violation of its obligations under the Charter and Security Council resolutions'.
- Resolution 271 dated 15 September 1969, in which the Security Council expressed grief 'at the extensive damage caused by arson to the Holy Al-Aqsa Mosque in Jerusalem' on 21 August 1969 'under the military occupation of Israel', and reaffirmed 'the established principle that acquisition of territory by military conquest is inadmissible', 'determines that the execrable act of desecration and profanation of the Holy Al-Aqsa Mosque

emphasises the immediate necessity of Israel's desisting from acting in violation' of previous resolutions and should rescind measures to annex Jerusalem, and called on Israel 'to observe the provisions of the Geneva Conventions and international law governing military occupation', and 'condemns Israel's failure to comply with UN resolutions on Jerusalem'.

- Resolution 279 dated 12 May 1970, in which the Security Council 'demands the immediate withdrawal of all Israeli armed forces from Lebanese territory'.
- Resolution 280 dated 19 May 1970, in which the Security Council condemned Israel for its large-scale, deliberate, carefully planned aggression against Lebanon, expressing the conviction 'that the Israeli military attack against Lebanon was premeditated and of a large scale and carefully planned in nature', recalled Resolution 279 'demanding the immediate withdrawal of all Israeli armed forces from Lebanese territory', and deplored Israel's violation of resolutions 262 and 270, 'condemns Israel for its premeditated military action in violation of its obligations under the Charter of the United Nations', and 'deplores the loss of life and damage to property inflicted as a result' of Israeli violations of Security Council resolutions.
- Resolution 285 dated 5 September 1970, in which the Security Council 'demands the complete and immediate withdrawal of all Israeli armed forces from Lebanese territory'.
- Resolution 298 dated 25 September 1971, in which the Security Council deplored Israel's changing of the status of Jerusalem.
- Resolution 313 dated 28 February 1972, in which the Security Council demanded that Israel stop attacks against Lebanon.
- Resolution 316 dated 26 June 1972, in which the Security Council condemned Israel for repeated attacks on Lebanon and demanded the immediate release of Syrian and Lebanese military and security personnel who had been abducted.
- Resolution 317 dated 21 July 1972, which expressed the Council's regret over Israel's failure to repatriate the Syrian and Lebanese military and security personnel referred to above, and called upon Israel to repatriate them without further delay.

- Resolution 332 dated 21 April 1973 condemned Israel for its repeated military attacks against Lebanon, and expressed the Council's regret over all the recent acts of violence which had led to the loss of innocent lives as well as having endangered civilian international aviation.
- Resolution 337 dated 15 August 1973, in which the Security Council condemned Israel for its violation of Lebanese sovereignty and territorial integrity and for the forcible diversion and seizure of a Lebanese civilian airliner from Lebanon's air space.
- Resolution 338 dated 22 October 1973, in which the Security Council called for a ceasefire in the Yom Kippur War and the implementation of Security Council Resolution 242 (1967) in all of its parts.
- Resolution 347 dated 24 April 24 1973, in which the Security Council condemned Israeli attacks on Lebanon, Israel's violation of Lebanon's territorial integrity and sovereignty, and called once more on the government of Israel to refrain from further military actions and threats against Lebanon.
- Resolution 368 dated 17 April 1975, in which the Security Council called on the parties involved in the prevailing state of tension in the Middle East to immediately implement Resolution 338.
- Resolution 425 dated 19 March 1978, in which the Security Council called upon Israel to immediately cease its military action against Lebanese territorial integrity and withdraw its forces forthwith from all Lebanese territory.
- Resolution 427 dated 3 May 1978, in which the Security Council 'calls on Israel to complete its withdrawal from Lebanon'.
- Resolution 446 dated 22 March 1979, in which the Security Council 'determines' that Israeli settlements are a 'serious obstruction' to peace and calls on Israel to abide by the Fourth Geneva Convention.
- Resolution 450 dated 14 June 1979, in which the Security Council called on Israel to stop attacking Lebanon and strongly

deplored acts of violence against Lebanon that had led to the displacement of civilians, including Palestinians, and brought about destruction and loss of innocent lives.

- Resolution 452 dated 20 July 1979, in which the Security Council called on Israeli occupation forces to cease operations involving the expansion of Israeli settlements in occupied Arab lands, including Jerusalem.
- Resolution 465 dated 1 March 1980, in which the Security Council deplored Israel's settlements and asked all member states not to assist Israel's settlements program.
- Resolution 467 dated 24 April 1980, in which the Security Council 'strongly deplores' Israel's military intervention in Lebanon.
- Resolution 468 dated 8 May 1980, which demanded that Israel (in its capacity as the occupying force) revoke all illegal measures (deportation) taken against the mayors of the townships of Hebron and Halhoul, and the Shari'a Magistrate of Hebron, and to facilitate their return.
- Resolution 469 dated 20 May 1980, in which the Security Council 'strongly deplores Israel's failure to observe the Council's order not to deport Palestinians', and demanded once again that Israel revoke all measures taken against the Palestinian leaders mentioned heretofore, and to facilitate their immediate repatriation so as to enable them to resume the duties the fulfilment of which they had been duly elected and appointed.
- Resolution 471 dated 5 June 1980, in which the Security Council expressed 'deep concern' at Israel's failure to abide by the Fourth Geneva Convention relative to the protection of civilian persons in time of war.
- Resolution 476 dated 30 June 1980, in which the Security Council 'reiterates' that Israel's claim to Jerusalem is 'null and void'.

- Resolution 478 dated 20 August 1980, in which the Security Council 'censures [Israel] in the strongest terms' for its claim to Jerusalem in its 'Basic Law'.
- Resolution 484 dated 19 December 1980, in which the Security Council 'declares its imperative' that Israel re-admit two deported Palestinian mayors.
- Resolution 487 dated 19 June 1981, in which the Security Council 'strongly condemns' Israel for its attack on Iraq's Osirak nuclear facility.
- Resolution 497 dated 17 December 1981, in which the Security Council decided that Israel's annexation of Syria's Golan Heights is 'null and void' and demands that Israel rescind its decision forthwith.
- Resolution 498 dated 18 December 1981, in which the Security Council called on Israel to withdraw from Lebanon.
- Resolution 501 dated 25 February 1982, in which the Security Council called on Israel to stop attacks against Lebanon and withdraw its troops.
- Resolution 508 dated 5 June 1982, in which the Security Council demanded an end to hostilities between Israel and the PLO taking place in Lebanon, and called for a ceasefire.
- Resolution 509 dated 6 June 1982, in which the Security Council 'demands that Israel withdraw its forces forthwith and unconditionally from Lebanon'.
- Resolution 515 dated 29 July 1982, in which the Security Council demanded that Israel lift its siege of Beirut and allow food supplies to be brought in.
- Resolution 516 dated 1 August 1982, in which the Security Council demanded an immediate cessation of military activities in Lebanon, noting violations of the ceasefire in Beirut.
- Resolution 517 dated 4 August 1982, in which the Security Council 'censures' Israel for failing to obey UN resolutions and demanded that Israel withdraw its forces from Lebanon.

- Resolution 518 dated 12 August 1982, in which the Security Council demanded that Israel cooperate fully with UNforces in Lebanon.
- Resolution 520 dated 17 September 1982, in which the Security Council condemned Israel's attack into West Beirut.
- Resolution 573 dated 4 October 1985, which condemned Israel's aggression against Tunis, which caused heavy losses of human life in addition to massive material losses, and urged member nations of the United Nation to take measures to prevent Israel from engaging in similar acts.
- Resolution 592 dated 8 December 1986, which condemned the Israeli army's having opened fire, thereby killing and wounding students at Bir Zeit University.
- Resolution 605 dated 22 December 1987, which condemned Israeli practices violating human rights of the Palestinian people in the occupied territories and asked Israel to adhere immediately and precisely to the Geneva accords related to the protection of civilians in time of war.
- Resolution 607 dated 5 January 1988, which asked that Israel refrain from deporting Palestinian civilians from the occupied territories.
- Resolution 608 dated 5 January 1988, which asked Israel to rescind the order to deport Palestinian civilians, and to ensure the repatriation of those already having been deported.
- Resolution 611 dated 25 April 1988, which condemned Israeli aggression against Tunis on 16 April 1988, an aggression which resulted in human loss of life.
- Resolution 636 dated 6 July 1989, which asked Israel to ensure the repatriation to the occupied territories of those who had been deported (eight Palestinian civilians as of 29 June 1989), and to desist from deporting any more Palestinian civilians.
- Resolution 641 dated 30 August 1989, which deplored Israel's continued deportation of Palestinian civilians (having deported five Palestinian civilians on 27 August 1989), and which asked

Israel to ensure the immediate repatriation of those thus far deported.

- Resolution 672 dated 12 October 1990, in which the Security Council condemned Israel for 'violence against Palestinians' at the Haram al-Sharif/Temple Mount.
- Resolution 673 dated 24 October 1990, in which the Security Council deplored Israel's refusal to cooperate with the United Nations.
- Resolution 681 dated 20 December 1990, in which the Security Council deplored Israel's resumption of the deportation of Palestinians.
- Resolution 694 dated 24 May 1991, in which the Security Council deplored Israel's deportation of Palestinians and called on it to ensure their safe and immediate return.
- Resolution 726 dated 6 January 1992, in which the Security Council 'strongly condemns' Israel's deportation of Palestinians.
- Resolution 799 dated 18 December 1992, in which the Security Council 'strongly condemns' Israel's deportation of 413 Palestinian civilians to Lebanon on 17 December 1992 from the territories occupied by Israel since 1967, including Jerusalem, in contravention of its obligations as the occupying power under the Fourth Geneva Convention of 1949, and called for their immediate return.
- Resolution 904 dated 18 March 1994 which condemned the Cave of the Patriarchs massacre.
- Resolution 1322 dated 7 October 2000 in which the Security Council deplored Ariel Sharon's visit to the Temple Mount and the violence that ensued.
- Resolution 1435 dated 24 September 2002 in which the Security Council demanded an end to Israeli measures in and around Ramallah, and an Israeli withdrawal to positions held before September 2000.
- Resolution 1701 dated 11 August 2006 in which the Security Council called for the 'immediate cessation by Israel of all

offensive military operations' against Lebanon and the full cessation of hostilities between Israel and Hezbollah.

- Resolution 1860 dated 9 January 2009 in which the Security Council called for the full cessation of war between Israel and Hamas.

UN Resolutions condemning Israeli aggression against Lebanon

- Resolution 262 dated 31 December 1968, in which the Security Council observed 'that the military action by the armed forces of Israel against the civil International Airport of Beirut was premeditated and of a large scale and carefully planned nature', and condemns Israel for the attack.
- Resolution 270 dated 26 August 1969, in which the Security Council 'condemns the premeditated air attack by Israel on villages in southern Lebanon in violation of its obligations under the Charter and Security Council resolutions'.
- Resolution 279 dated 12 May 1970, in which the Security Council 'demands the immediate withdrawal of all Israeli forces from Lebanese territory'.
- Resolution 280 dated 19 May 1970, in which the Security Council condemned Israel for its large-scale, deliberate, carefully planned aggression against Lebanon, expressing the conviction 'that the Israeli military attack against Lebanon was premeditated and of a large scale and carefully planned in nature', recalled Resolution 279 'demanding the immediate withdrawal of all Israeli armed forces from Lebanese territory', deplored Israel's violation of resolutions 262 and 270, 'condemns Israel for its premeditated military action in violation of its obligations under the Charter of the United Nations', and 'deplores the loss of life and damage to property inflicted as a result' of Israeli violations of Security Council resolutions.
- Resolution 285 dated 5 September 1970, in which the Security Council 'demands the complete and immediate withdrawal of all Israeli armed forces from Lebanese territory'.

- Resolution 313 dated 28 February 1972, in which the Security Council demanded that Israel stop attacks against Lebanon.
- Resolution 316 dated 26 June 1972, in which the Security Council condemned Israel for repeated attacks on Lebanon and demanded the immediate release of Syrian and Lebanese military and security personnel who had been abducted.
- Resolution 317 dated 21 July 1972, which expressed the Council's regret over Israel's failure to repatriate the Syrian and Lebanese military and security personnel referred to above, and called upon Israel to repatriate them without further delay.
- Resolution 332 dated 21 April 1973, which condemned Israel for its repeated military attacks against Lebanon, and expressed the Council's regret over all the recent acts of violence which had led to the loss of innocent lives and which had endangered civilian international aviation.
- Resolution 337 dated 15 August 1973, in which the Security Council condemned Israel for its violation of Lebanese sovereignty and territorial integrity and for the forcible diversion and seizure of a Lebanese civilian airliner from Lebanon's air space.
- Resolution 347 dated 24 April 1973, in which the Security Council condemned Israeli attacks on Lebanon, Israel's violation of Lebanon's territorial integrity and sovereignty and called once more on the government of Israel to refrain from further military actions and threats against Lebanon.
- Resolution 425 dated 19 March 1978, in which the Security Council called upon Israel to immediately cease its military action against Lebanese territorial integrity and forthwith withdraw its forces from all Lebanese territory.
- Resolution 427 dated 3 May 1978, in which the Security Council 'calls on Israel to complete its withdrawal from Lebanon'.
- Resolution 450 dated 14 June 1979, in which the Security Council called on Israel to stop attacking Lebanon and strongly deplored acts of violence against Lebanon that led to the

displacement of civilians, including Palestinians, and brought about destruction and loss of innocent lives.

- Resolution 459 dated 19 December 1979, in which the Security Council reaffirmed its determination, in the event of continuing obstruction of the mandate of the Force (United Nations Interim Force in Lebanon [UNIFIL]), to examine practical ways and means in accordance with relevant provisions of the Charter of the United Nations to secure the full implementation of Resolution 425.
- Resolution 467 dated 24 April 1980, in which the Security Council 'strongly deplores' Israel's military intervention in Lebanon.
- Resolution 483 dated 18 December 1980, in which the Security Council reaffirmed its determination, in the event of continuing obstruction by Israel of the mandate of UNIFIL, to examine practical ways and means to secure the full implementation of Resolution 425.
- Resolution 481 dated 19 June 1981, in which the Security Council condemned all actions contrary to the provisions of the above-mentioned resolutions that prevented the full implementation of UNIFIL's mandate, causing death, injury and destruction to the civilian population as well as among the peace-keeping force.
- Resolution 498 dated 18 December 1981, in which the Security Council called on Israel to withdraw from Lebanon.
- Resolution 501 dated 25 February 1982, in which the Security Council called on Israel to stop attacks against Lebanon and withdraw its troops.
- Resolution 508 dated 5 June 1982, in which the Security Council demanded an end to hostilities between Israel and the PLO taking place in Lebanon, and called for a ceasefire.
- Resolution 509 dated 6 June 1982, in which the Security Council 'demands that Israel withdraw its forces forthwith and unconditionally from Lebanon'.

- Resolution 515 dated 29 July 1982, in which the Security Council demanded that Israel lift its siege of Beirut and allow food supplies to be brought in.
- Resolution 516 dated 1 August 1982, in which the Security Council demanded an immediate cessation of military activities in Lebanon, noting violations of the ceasefire in Beirut.
- Resolution 517 dated 4 August 1982, in which the Security Council 'censures' Israel for failing to obey UN resolutions and demanded that Israel withdraw its forces from Lebanon.
- Resolution 518 dated 12 August 1982, in which the Security Council demanded that Israel cooperate fully with UN forces in Lebanon.
- Resolution 520 dated 17 September 1982, in which the Security Council condemned Israel's attack into West Beirut.
- Resolution 555 dated 12 October 1984, in which the Security Council reiterated that the United Nations Interim Force in Lebanon should fully implement its mandate as defined in resolutions 425, 426 and all other relevant resolutions.
- Resolution 587 dated 23 September 1986, in which the Security Council notes with regret that UNIFIL, whose mandate has been renewed for the twenty-first time, has so far been prevented from fulfilling the task entrusted to it.
- Resolution 799 dated 18 December 1992, in which the Security Council 'strongly condemns' Israel's deportation of 413 Palestinian civilians to Lebanon on 17 December 1992, from the territories occupied by Israel since 1967, including Jerusalem, in contravention of its obligations as the occupying power under the Fourth Geneva Convention of 1949, and called for their immediate return.
- Resolution 1701 dated 11 August 2006 in which the Security Council called for the 'immediate cessation by Israel of all offensive military operations' against Lebanon and the full cessation of hostilities between Israel and Hezbollah, and called upon the government of Israel to withdraw all of its forces from southern Lebanon.

3. Blind justice: Israeli terrorism and international law's double standards

Why is it that the Israelis can assassinate Palestinian leaders at will, use live ammunition against stone-throwing Palestinian children, destroy Palestinian homes, deport Palestinian civilians, use white phosphorous against Palestinian civilians, and not be branded terrorists, while Palestinians fighting to end Israeli occupation of their ancestral land and to achieve statehood are accused of being 'terrorists'?

How are the acts perpetrated by the Israelis any different from any other terrorist acts, especially when Israelis are the ones who initiated the violence and assassinations by unlawfully occupying Arab land? Palestinians who resist Israeli occupation are dubbed 'terrorists' by Israel, while Israel's violent repression is always in 'self-defence' and, in the post-11 September attacks, part of the global 'war on terror'.

As for the terrorist actions committed by Israel that have claimed the lives of thousands of defenceless Palestinian civilians since the start of the *Intifada*, they do not go beyond being merely described as 'provocative' or 'counter-productive'. It is this twisted, distorted and totally biased logic that forces otherwise moderate Palestinians to resort to violence as the only means to end Israel's state terrorism and the ensuing tension, instability, and economic and social hardships in the occupied territories.

It should not be forgotten that prominent figures in the Israeli government were notorious Zionist terrorists at one time or another, including Menachem Begin, Itzhak Shamir, and Ariel Sharon. It is no secret that Begin and Shamir led the Irgun and Stern Zionist terrorist organisations, a fact completely overlooked today by international law and the international community. Thus, Israel's accusation that the PLO is a 'terrorist' organisation seems preposterous, given the Jewish entity's prolific record of terrorist activities.

This leaves us to ponder whether the fact that Israel has never been accused of practicing terrorism really indicates that a qualitative difference exists between its actions and those perpetrated by Palestinian resistance groups. Israel's great advantage is that it is a state, and state terrorism has always been disregarded by international law—with a few possible exceptions — while the Palestinians are non-state actors and hence potential 'terrorists'.

To this day, states are permitted to freely practise terrorism, whereas terrorist acts carried out by individuals or groups are quickly branded as such. This fact has dangerous repercussions, for state terrorism — and its unholy offspring, state-sponsored terrorism - is a breeding ground for international terrorism, and failing to take steps aimed at ending it undermines international law's legitimacy and credibility.

4. Israel's state terrorism under the cover of 'self-defence'

Israel has been practicing terrorism in the West Bank and the Gaza Strip ever since it occupied these Arab territories in 1967. According to Human Rights Watch, during the *Intifada*, Israeli undercover units notoriously known as death squads penetrated Palestinian settlements, killing Palestinians by means of summary executions: the unit would locate a victim, and without attempting to arrest him, shot in order to kill. HRW estimates that these units killed hundreds of Palestinians over the course of the *Intifada*.

The actions and methods used by these undercover units and the objectives Israel wanted to achieve by these 'targeted killings', i.e. Israel's assassination policy, completely conform to the definition of terrorism.

Moreover, the use of live ammunition by Israeli occupation forces against stone-throwing Palestinian youths and children, the Israeli army's arbitrary demolition of Palestinian homes, its pursuit of the aggressive policy of building settlements and enlarging existing ones, land confiscation, the Shin Bet's (Israel's secret service) extensive use of torture and other inhuman treatment against arbitrarily detained Palestinians (some of them children under the age of eight!), the forced displacement or deportation of entire families as a form of ethnic cleansing, the economic blockade of self-governing Palestinian areas, the denial of access to Red Cross ambulances carrying wounded Palestinian civilians and medical aid, and the Israeli system's unabashed ethnic, social, cultural, and religious discrimination against Arab-Israelis are all but a few examples of the Jewish state's ongoing political, military, social, and religious terrorism against the Palestinian people.

Yet despite all these clear acts of terrorism, from the Israeli point of view, violence committed by Israel against Palestinians is always 'defensive', and part of the 'war on terrorism', and hence 'terrorist' has become a word abused mainly by Israel, especially since 11 September, to label anyone opposed to its colonialist and expansionist policies.

Accordingly, Israel's military occupation of the West Bank and Gaza, its routine use of torture, its arbitrary demolition of homes, and its policy of political assassinations are not, in Israel's eyes, examples of terrorism, but are simply necessary for 'self-defence' and Israel's sacrosanct 'security'; the Jewish entity is trying to camouflage its state-sponsored terrorism as defensive measures.

If Palestinians use violence in resisting Israeli occupation, they always do so at a far lower level — given their limited means I — and yet it is always regarded as 'terrorism' by the Israelis. Similarly, when Israel occupied Lebanon throughout the 1980s and 1990s in violation of UN Security Council resolutions, the violence of that occupation was in 'self-defence', and the Lebanese National Resistance to that occupation was labelled terrorism. This was a ludicrous claim, since it is Israel which to this day still occupies parts of Lebanese territory, and refuses to deliver the maps of minefields which were laid in South Lebanon and the Western Bekaa by the Israeli army and its proxy militia, the 'South Lebanon Army'.

Appendix II: United Nations Security Council Resolutions Pertaining to Terrorism

- Resolution 2083 dated 17 December 2012
- Resolution 2082 dated 17 December 2012
- Resolution 2055 dated 29 June 2012
- Resolution 1989 dated 17 June 2011
- Resolution 1977 dated 20 April 2011
- Resolution 1963 dated 20 December 2010
- Resolution 1904 dated 17 December 2009
- Resolution 1887 dated 24 September 2009
- Resolution 1822 dated 30 June 2008
- Resolution 1810 dated 25 April 2008
- Resolution 1805 dated 20 March 2008
- Resolution 1787 dated 10 December 2007
- Resolution 1735 dated 22 December 2006
- Resolution 1730 dated 19 December 2006
- Resolution 1624 dated 14 September 2005
- Resolution 1617 dated 29 July 2005
- Resolution 1566 dated 8 October 2004
- Resolution 1556 dated 30 July 2004
- Resolution 1540 dated 28 April 2004
- Resolution 1535 dated 26 March 2004

- Resolution 1526 dated 30 January 2004
- Resolution 1456 dated 20 January 2003
- Resolution 1455 dated 17 January 2003
- Resolution 1452 dated 20 December 2002
- Resolution 1390 dated 28 January 2002
- Resolution 1388 dated 15 January 2002
- Resolution 1377 dated 12 November 2001
- Resolution 1373 dated 28 September 2001
- Resolution 1368 dated 12 September 2001
- Resolution 1363 dated 30 June 2001
- Resolution 1333 dated 19 December 2000
- Resolution 1269 dated 19 October 1999
- Resolution 1267 dated 15 October 1999
- Resolution 579 dated 18 December 1985
- Resolution 286 dated 9 September 1970

References

This book is based on a study entitled *Defining Terrorism: Conditions and Criteria for Consensus - Draft Proposal for a Universal Definition of Terrorism*, which was submitted by the author on 6 February 2002 to the Lebanese Ministry of Foreign Affairs and Emigrants. The study was sent as a circular by the Ministry to all Lebanese diplomatic missions in the world as a reference.

This book also contains information taken from a report entitled *Israeli violations of International Law and Human Rights in Lebanon: 1978-1998*, submitted by the author on 18 April 1998 to the Lebanese Ministry of Foreign Affairs and Emigrants. The report was sent by the Ministry to the Lebanese Permanent Mission to the United Nations in New York and submitted by the Mission to the UN General Assembly on 18 November 1998, on the occasion of the fiftieth anniversary of the Universal Declaration of Human Rights and circulated as a document of the General Assembly.

Additional sources:

- Articles published in the Lebanese daily newspaper, the *Daily Star*
- The UN Charter and UN resolutions.
- International terrorism conventions
- The Geneva Conventions of 1949
- The Oxford Dictionary
- Statutes of the International Criminal Court (ICC)
- Reports of Human Rights Watch (HRW)
- Reports of Amnesty International
- Reports of the International Committee of the Red Cross (ICRC)

- The following articles on terrorism (online):
    - 'International versus Internal Armed Conflict' by Steven R. Ratner, available at www.crimesofwar.org
    - 'Palestine and Terrorism' by Robert Jensen, available at www.commondreams.org/views01/0308-02.htm
    - 'Defining Terrorism and Assigning the Label' by Neve Gordon, available at oznik.com/words/010923.html
    - 'Defining Terrorism: One Country's "Terrorist" is Another Country's "Freedom Fighter". Can we Tell the Difference?' by Holger Jensen (no longer available)
    - 'Defining Terrorism' by Mohammad sid-Ahmed, available at weekly.ahram.org.eg/1999/439/op3.htm
    - 'Rogue State: Israeli Violations of U.N. Security Council Resolutions' by Jeremy R. Hammond, available at www.foreignpolicyjournal.com/2010/01/27/rogue-state-israeli-violations-of-u-n-security-council-resolutions/

Index

T

U

W

Y

ABOUT THE AUTHOR

Ambassador, Philosopher, Scholar, Author, Poet. Dr. Taha Audi holds a PHD in Philosophy from the Sorbonne University, Paris, and a Master's degree in Political Science from the American University. A senior career diplomat, she has previously served in Geneva, Paris, and Tokyo, and was appointed Consul General in New York in 2019. In addition to her diplomatic and academic careers, Dr Audi is also an internationally published author of several books, translated into several languages, and numerous articles, in the fields of Philosophy, Spirituality, Politics, Poetry, and Literature, as well as several works on International Law and Organizations, most of which were adopted as official documents by the UN. Versed in philosophy and mysticism, the author espouses a spiritual worldview and believes that man's ultimate purpose and vocation in life is the fulfilment of his divine nature and destiny. Dr Taha speaks fluent English, French and German.

ALSO BY THE AUTHOR

- Rousseau, le dernier bon sauvage, ou l'âme de la République ("Rousseau, the Last Good Savage, or the Soul of the Republic") (Dr Taha's PHD Thesis, Sorbonne, Paris, 2022).

- *Fallen Suns, Rising Stars – A Novel about Second Chances* (Literary Talents, Amazon, New York, 2019).
- *Twelve Resolutions for a Happy Life – A Manual of Happiness* (Numen Press, Australia, 2015; second edition: Manticore Press, Australia, 2022).
- *Verses of Light* (Arktos, London, 2014).
- *The Epic of Arya – In Search of the Sacred Light* (Author House, USA, 2009; second edition: Arktos, London, 2016).
- *Nietzsche, Prophet of Nazism: The Cult of the Superman* (Author House, USA, 2005). The book was translated into Portuguese and published in Brazil.
- *Le Dieu à Venir de Nietzsche, ou la Rédemption du Divin* (Editions Connaissances et Savoirs, Paris, 2005). The book was translated into English under the title Nietzsche's Coming God, or the Redemption of the Divine, and published by Arktos in London in 2013. It was also translated into Spanish.

Facebook page: Ambassador Dr Abir Taha – Author.

OTHER BOOKS PUBLISHED BY ARKTOS

Virginia Abernethy	*Born Abroad*
Sri Dharma Pravartaka Acharya	*The Dharma Manifesto*
Joakim Andersen	*Rising from the Ruins*
Winston C. Banks	*Excessive Immigration*
Alain de Benoist	*Beyond Human Rights* *Carl Schmitt Today* *The Ideology of Sameness* *The Indo-Europeans* *Manifesto for a European Renaissance* *On the Brink of the Abyss* *The Problem of Democracy* *Runes and the Origins of Writing* *View from the Right* (vol. 1–3)
Armand Berger	*Tolkien, Europe, and Tradition*
Arthur Moeller van den Bruck	*Germany's Third Empire*
Matt Battaglioli	*The Consequences of Equality*
Kerry Bolton	*The Perversion of Normality* *Revolution from Above* *Yockey: A Fascist Odyssey*
Isac Boman	*Money Power*
Charles William Dailey	*The Serpent Symbol in Tradition*
Ricardo Duchesne	*Faustian Man in a Multicultural Age*
Alexander Dugin	*Ethnos and Society* *Ethnosociology* *Eurasian Mission* *The Fourth Political Theory* *The Great Awakening vs the Great Reset* *Last War of the World-Island* *Political Platonism* *Putin vs Putin* *The Rise of the Fourth Political Theory* *Templars of the Proletariat* *The Theory of a Multipolar World*
Edward Dutton	*Race Differences in Ethnocentrism*
Mark Dyal	*Hated and Proud*
Clare Ellis	*The Blackening of Europe*
Koenraad Elst	*Return of the Swastika*
Julius Evola	*The Bow and the Club* *Fascism Viewed from the Right* *A Handbook for Right-Wing Youth* *Metaphysics of Power* *Metaphysics of War* *The Myth of the Blood* *Notes on the Third Reich* *The Path of Cinnabar* *Recognitions*

OTHER BOOKS PUBLISHED BY ARKTOS

	A Traditionalist Confronts Fascism
Guillaume Faye	*Archeofuturism* *Archeofuturism 2.0* *The Colonisation of Europe* *Convergence of Catastrophes* *Ethnic Apocalypse* *A Global Coup* *Prelude to War* *Sex and Deviance* *Understanding Islam* *Why We Fight*
Daniel S. Forrest	*Suprahumanism*
Andrew Fraser	*Dissident Dispatches* *Reinventing Aristocracy in the Age of Woke Capital* *The WASP Question*
Génération Identitaire	*We are Generation Identity*
Peter Goodchild	*The Taxi Driver from Baghdad* *The Western Path*
Paul Gottfried	*War and Democracy*
Petr Hampl	*Breached Enclosure*
Porus Homi Havewala	*The Saga of the Aryan Race*
Lars Holger Holm	*Hiding in Broad Daylight* *Homo Maximus* *Incidents of Travel in Latin America* *The Owls of Afrasiab*
Richard Houck	*Liberalism Unmasked*
A. J. Illingworth	*Political Justice*
Alexander Jacob	*De Naturae Natura*
Jason Reza Jorjani	*Artemis Unveiled* *Closer Encounters* *Faustian Futurist* *Iranian Leviathan* *Lovers of Sophia* *Novel Folklore* *Prometheism* *Promethean Pirate* *Prometheus and Atlas* *Uber Man* *World State of Emergency*
Henrik Jonasson	*Sigmund*
Edgar Julius Jung	*The Significance of the German Revolution*
Ruuben Kaalep & August Meister	*Rebirth of Europe*
Roderick Kaine	*Smart and SeXy*
Peter King	*Here and Now*

OTHER BOOKS PUBLISHED BY ARKTOS

	Keeping Things Close
	On Modern Manners
James Kirkpatrick	*Conservatism Inc.*
Ludwig Klages	*The Biocentric Worldview*
	Cosmogonic Reflections
	The Science of Character
Andrew Korybko	*Hybrid Wars*
Pierre Krebs	*Guillaume Faye: Truths & Tributes*
	Fighting for the Essence
Julien Langella	*Catholic and Identitarian*
John Bruce Leonard	*The New Prometheans*
Stephen Pax Leonard	*The Ideology of Failure*
	Travels in Cultural Nihilism
William S. Lind	*Reforging Excalibur*
	Retroculture
Pentti Linkola	*Can Life Prevail?*
H. P. Lovecraft	*The Conservative*
Norman Lowell	*Imperium Europa*
Richard Lynn	*Sex Differences in Intelligence*
John MacLugash	*The Return of the Solar King*
Charles Maurras	*The Future of the Intelligentsia & For a French Awakening*
John Harmon McElroy	*Agitprop in America*
Michael O'Meara	*Guillaume Faye and the Battle of Europe*
	New Culture, New Right
Michael Millerman	*Beginning with Heidegger*
Maurice Muret	*The Greatness of Elites*
Brian Anse Patrick	*The NRA and the Media*
	Rise of the Anti-Media
	The Ten Commandments of Propaganda
	Zombology
Tito Perdue	*The Bent Pyramid*
	Journey to a Location
	Lee
	Morning Crafts
	Philip
	The Sweet-Scented Manuscript
	William's House (vol. 1–4)
John K. Press	*The True West vs the Zombie Apocalypse*
Raido	*A Handbook of Traditional Living* (vol. 1–2)
Claire Rae Randall	*The War on Gender*
Steven J. Rosen	*The Agni and the Ecstasy*
	The Jedi in the Lotus
Nicholas Rooney	*Talking to the Wolf*

OTHER BOOKS PUBLISHED BY ARKTOS

Richard Rudgley	*Barbarians* *Essential Substances* *Wildest Dreams*
Ernst von Salomon	*It Cannot Be Stormed* *The Outlaws*
Werner Sombart	*Traders and Heroes*
Piero San Giorgio	*CBRN* *Giuseppe* *Survive the Economic Collapse*
Sri Sri Ravi Shankar	*Celebrating Silence* *Know Your Child* *Management Mantras* *Patanjali Yoga Sutras* *Secrets of Relationships*
George T. Shaw (ed.)	*A Fair Hearing*
Fenek Solère	*Kraal* *Reconquista*
Oswald Spengler	*The Decline of the West* *Man and Technics*
Richard Storey	*The Uniqueness of Western Law*
Tomislav Sunic	*Against Democracy and Equality* *Homo Americanus* *Postmortem Report* *Titans are in Town*
Askr Svarte	*Gods in the Abyss*
Hans-Jürgen Syberberg	*On the Fortunes and Misfortunes of Art in Post-War Germany*
Abir Taha	*Defining Terrorism* *The Epic of Arya* (2nd ed.) *Nietzsche's Coming God, or the Redemption of the Divine* *Verses of Light*
Jean Thiriart	*Europe: An Empire of 400 Million*
Bal Gangadhar Tilak	*The Arctic Home in the Vedas*
Dominique Venner	*For a Positive Critique* *The Shock of History*
Hans Vogel	*How Europe Became American*
Markus Willinger	*A Europe of Nations* *Generation Identity*
Alexander Wolfheze	*Alba Rosa* *Rupes Nigra*